# Piet
# Oudolf

## Landscapes

## pes

**Written with
Noël Kingsbury**

# in Landscapes

Acknowledgments

My thanks to the
following people:

ANJA
Mary Armstrong
Sierra Bainbridge
Bridget Baines
Massimo Benetazzo
Kina Bergdahl
Monika Bergerhoff
Marina Bertaggio
Heinz Joseph Bickmann
Massimiliano Bigarello
Harry Birckmayer
Pierre Blondea
Irma Boom
Piet and Karin Boon
Serge Bottagisio and Agnes
Decoux
Jan Bremer
James Bruv
Patrick Calluna
Paul Casteleijn
Isabel Castilla
Imogen Checketts
Sam Chermayeff
Marcus Chilton-Jones
John Coke
James Corner
Ulrike Crespo
Colin Crosbie
Ursula Cullinan
Rick Darke
Joshua David
Jennifer Davit
Erik A. de Jong
Roy Diblik
Dinie and Lammert
Emschergenossenschaft
Elisabeth Fain

Mellissa Fischer
Kurt Fortin
Jim Gardiner
El and Aad Geelings
G.G.N Landscape Architects
Judith Giesberts
Elizabeth Gilmore
Anthony Glossop
Sigrid Gray
Terry Guen
Kathryn Gustafson
Jennifer Guthrie
Jan Halsema
Robert Hammond
Debbie Harrison
Wilhemina Hellman
Erik and Petra Hesmerg
The Staff of the High Line
Verena Holtzgethan
Eelco Hooftman
Nahyun Hwang
Robert Israel
Thomas Kellein
Richard Kennedy
Eun Young Kim
Michael King
Noël Kingsbury
Pat Kirschner
Steven Lagerstrom
Lady Caroline and
Sir Charles Legard
Paul Legeckis
Hélène Lesger
Christian Liaigre
Colleen Lockovitch
Manuela Lucadazio
Bill Makins
Marijana Mance
Tim Marshall
Bob Marzilli
Stefan Mattson
Florian Matzner

Oisin May
Petra McCauliffe
Eric Mead
Lucy Mooney
Peter Mullan
Kristen Newman
Shannon Nichol
Phyllis Odessey
Sebastian Ortmann
Herbert and Ellie Oudshoorn
Pensthorpe Nature Reserve
Mark Pledger
Jef Poor
Warrie Price
H. Reisman
Rene Rheims
Maura Rockastle
Frans Roozen
Tom Ryan
Kari Sallinen
Nigel Sampey
Michael Satke
Cassian and Bettina Schmidt
Climmy Schneider
G. Schwartz
Kazuyo Sejima
Jason Shute
Laura Star
Tom Stuart-Smith
Lisa Switkin
Karin Tamir
Klaus and Ulrike Thews
Steve Thompson
Maureena Toft
Abraham Tung
Ed Uhlir
Jacqueline van der Kloet
Toria van Ittersum
Marcus and Annabelle von
Oeynhausen-Siertorpff
Viviane and Edward
Michael Walker

William Wallace
Claire Weisz
Finbarr Williamson
Tom Windsor
Pieter and Alma
The G. Wolf Family
Mark Yoes
Heeyeun Yoon

and everyone else that helped
to get these projects realized.

Library of Congress Cataloging-in-Publication Data

Oudolf, Piet. Landscapes in landscapes /
by Piet Oudolf ; written with Noël Kingsbury. —
1st ed. p. cm.
ISBN 978-1-58093-292-9 (hardcover)
1. Gardens—Europe—Pictorial works.
2. Gardens—United States—Pictorial works.
I. Kingsbury, Noël.
II. Title.
SB465.O93 2010, 712'.2—dc22, 2010024751
Printed in China

10 9 8 7 6 5 4 3 2 1
First edition

www.monacellipress.com

Designed by Irma Boom

# Contents

# Foreword

*"The High Line should be preserved, untouched, as a wilderness area. No doubt you will ruin it. So it goes."*

This comment was handed in on a public input card after our 2003 High Line Ideas Competition and I've kept it pinned above my desk ever since. It scared me because I believed it could come true.

The High Line was a serendipitous wildscape when Joshua David and I first walked on it in the summer of 1999. Grasses, wildflowers, and small trees had taken over the surface of the abandoned elevated rail line. It was unplanned and untended, and that's what made it so special. My biggest fear was that turning it into a park would spur the loss of a magical, accidental landscape thriving in relative secret above the West Side of Manhattan. At first we hoped to keep it as it was, to preserve that wild state and to simply run a path down the middle of the railway. We soon learned that would be impossible. In order to open it to the public we needed to make repairs, and that meant removing what remained of the ties, the rails, and the ballast—and everything growing on top of them. I knew we could not replicate what had taken nature decades to unfold. Even after I saw the plans that Piet Oudolf developed with our design team, led by James Corner Field Operations, schemes that drew inspiration from the palette of volunteer plants found growing there, I was anxious that the new plantings would fall short of that romantic original landscape. It was not until after the park opened in the summer of 2010 and I could see how the High Line's blooms, grasses, and foliage changed every few weeks that I realized that Piet had not only recaptured that original magic, but that he had also created a new landscape that had the ability to alter the way people feel and how they act.

People do not walk slowly in New York. They rarely stroll. But they do on the High Line. Couples hold hands. Parents remark upon the various plants as they use the High Line to walk their children leisurely to and from school. Piet's landscape allows people to breathe easier—not for its manicured beauty, but for its ability to change as nature does.

The range and complexity of Piet's plantings give visitors reasons to come back again and again. Week after week, month after month, they are lessons in discovery. Where many garden designers think of landscapes in terms of the four main seasons, Piet's seasons are broken into seasons. His aspirations may be ecological in nature, but he works like a painter. He dials color up, and then back, sometimes massing bold swatches of color that lead your eye through the landscape, at other times subtly dotting little spectral islands into larger seas of grasses. The complexity of these combinations is heightened as he employs various and distinct aspects of a single plant's annual cycle for various purposes throughout a single year. His plants are actors playing multiple roles—the blue stars that entertain with small, pale blue flowers in May return with a bold statement when their foliage turns a brilliant gold in the fall.

With Oudolf, it's not just about flowers. His landscapes, while certainly floral, are meant to confound the "what's-in-bloom?" mentality that drives much of the garden world. Plants are prized for their flowers, yes, but also for their height—and the gradual pace pursued to achieve their eventual statures—for their foliage's texture and color in spring and summer as well as fall and winter, for their fruit or seed-heads, and even for the color of their stems. Whether the plants are ascendant or in decline, all of their features have roles to play, through the year. And it all appears so disarmingly simple.

Of course, you do not need to think about any of this when you walk through one of his landscapes. But I suspect that you will be moved, or inspired, or maybe you will just feel better—even if you don't know why. There is something at work that will, I think, connect you to the kind of feelings I experienced when I walked on the High Line that first time—a belief in the ability of such spaces to change the way we see the world, and perhaps each other, season after season, all year long.

**Robert Hammond**
Co-founder
Friends of the High Line

# 350 m²

This project marks a transition phase between Oudolf's earliest work—when "all garden design was influenced by Mien Ruys," he says—and his later work, when he set out on a truly independent path. Designed for close friends, this garden responds to a common type of urban site: a long, narrow strip behind a townhouse.

Mien Ruys (1904–1999) was one of the most prolific and influential garden designers of the twentieth century. She began designing gardens in the 1920s, leaving a portfolio of around three thousand designs by the time she died. Her style was firmly in the modernist tradition, yet she used planting in a way that was ornamental as well as functional. From the early 1990s on, Oudolf's work began to engage more with his own personal garden flora—much of which he grew himself at Hummelo—and less with the architectural look of the Mien Ruys school. This 350-square-meter garden is a good illustration of that. The Hesmerg Garden is dominated by a diagonally aligned pattern of box running almost the whole length of the garden, contrasted by a border running the entire length of the garden wall. The border has a few rhododendrons but is essentially herbaceous, with varieties of *Hosta*, *Aconitum*, *Persicaria*—all favorites of Oudolf's—and the 2.2-meter-high *Eupatorium maculatum* 'Atropurpureum,' which is the kind of plant few designers were using in town gardens at the time this one was developed.

Adding to the luxurious atmosphere, the house wall and the wall that runs along one side of the garden support a variety of climbers: wisteria, the large-leaved Japanese vine *Vitis coignetiae*, and the familiar *Parthenocissus tricuspidata*. The climbers and perennials create a dramatic juxtaposition with the clipped box, illustrating that two very different styles of planting design can be successful in the same garden.

Hesmerg Garden, Sneek, The Netherlands, 1993

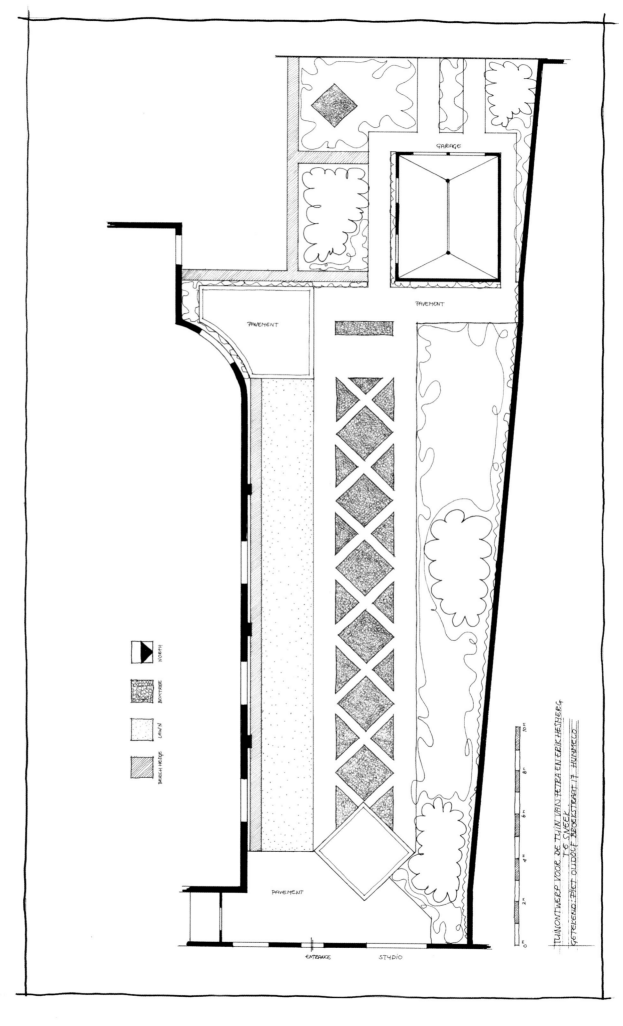

# 1,000 m²

This garden for a residence near Barcelona is the first project Oudolf has undertaken that is not located in a cool, temperate zone. Enclosed by hedges of *Cupressus sempervirens* on two sides, and by a wall and the house itself on the others, this 1,200-square-meter garden is in some ways classically Mediterranean. The plant selection contains many of the familiar low, hummocky, gray-leaved shrubs that define the character of the vegetation of this region. On the other hand, it is radically different from the vast majority of Mediterranean gardens, so many of which are still bound to an outmoded neoclassicism. The style here is firmly naturalistic, in that elements of local natural landscapes—the low shrubs and grasses—are featured. Irrigation is intended to be minimal, so each plant was selected for its drought tolerance.

While the inspiration for this garden is firmly derived from the region itself, the mix of plants was chosen with an eye to creating a long season of interest, so several species found here originate from the drier areas of the North American prairie. The bulk of the garden features combinations of plants, usually mixing at least one grass with a flowering perennial or two, or a perennial and a shrub. There are some eight combinations in all. Around the perimeter, narrow beds contain shrubs included for their spring or early-summer flower, underplanted with the dark-leaved grasslike plant *Ophiopogon planiscarpus* 'Nigrescens.'

This may be a small garden, but it marks an important evolution in planting design for Mediterranean climates, which has, to date, seen relatively little contemporary development.

Barcelona Garden, Barcelona, Spain, 2007

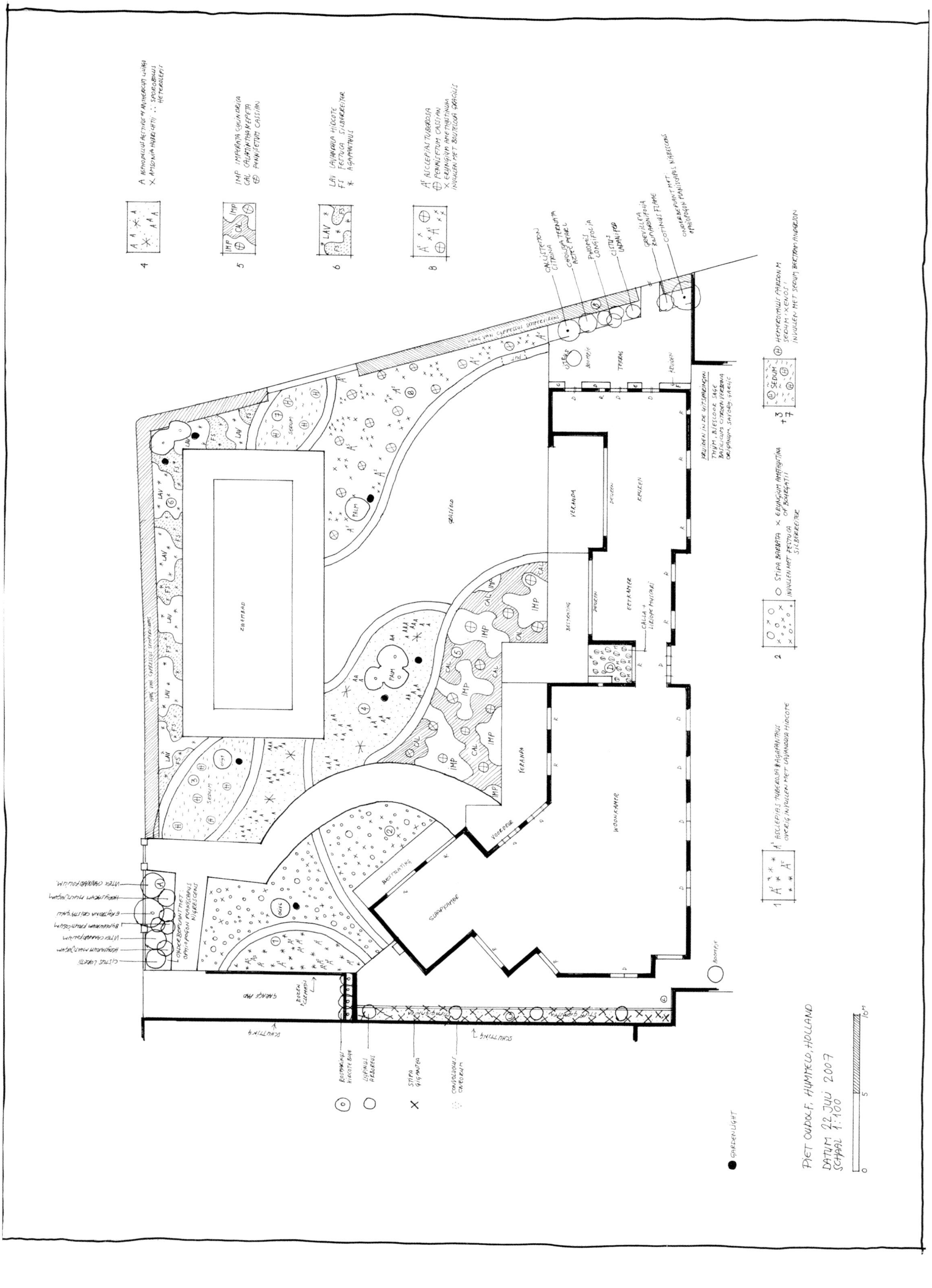

PIET OUDOLF, HUMMELO, HOLLAND
DATUM 22 JULI 2007
SCHAAL 1:100
WOONKAMER
SLAAPKAMER
EETKAMER
KEUKEN
VERANDA
ZWEMBAD
TERRAS
GARDENLIGHT

# 1,200 m²

As a property in Germany's Schleswig-Holstein region near the Danish border, this site encompasses many features of traditional farms of the north European plain: brick buildings and steep thatched roofs. Its newly constructed house, however, is a complete and very contemporary contrast—a structure of gray weathered wood. Oudolf acted purely as a designer in this case; the clients performed all the implementation themselves, with the work carried out in stages over several years.

There are perennials in this 1,200-square-meter garden area, but their role feels like a subsidiary one; Oudolf works in a more architectural vein here. The hedging instead plays the key part in establishing mood, and creates a series of separate areas that offer a variety of extremely different spatial experiences.

The living room of the new house looks out through a screen of pleached beech and over a terrace, beyond which is a formal planting of silver pear (*Pyrus salicifolia*), kept clipped to 1.2 meters high, and four varieties of blue salvia, which flower twice a year, once in May/June and again in September if cut back in July. A path leading from the old house cuts across the axis of this vista and leads into an area dominated by a circle-shaped pond and surrounded by yew hedging. This acts as the centerpiece of a "perennial meadow" planting, where the maximum height of the foliage is around 1 meter; varieties of sedum, hemerocallis, rodgersia, perovskia, and amsonia provide color, texture, and structure over a long season. To one side, a new yew hedge is given character with a low cut and an undulating top. Beyond the pond and meadow garden, an outer zone of yew and mixed beech/*Cornus mas* hedging is sculpted into a coolly minimalist space—a corridor curves gently between high hedges, with native woody plants clipped into rounded shapes at one end. The client has also trimmed the original boundary hedge of traditional hedging plants such as hawthorn, hazel, hornbeam, and dogwood, into an irregular hummocky wave, in the manner of the boundary hedge at Oudolf's own garden in Hummelo.

Clipped woody plants are only one aspect of the architectural minimalism established in this garden, though. There is also a group of grass *Deschampsia cespitosa* between the entrance gate and the new house and a broad edging of Japanese grass *Hakonechloa macra* around the base of the house. The latter grass has leaves that grow at such an angle that it looks as if the plant has been neatly combed. These grass blocks and the clipped hedges produce a highly effective contrast to the garden's central zone of perennial exuberance.

Thews Garden, Faulück, Germany, 1996–2006

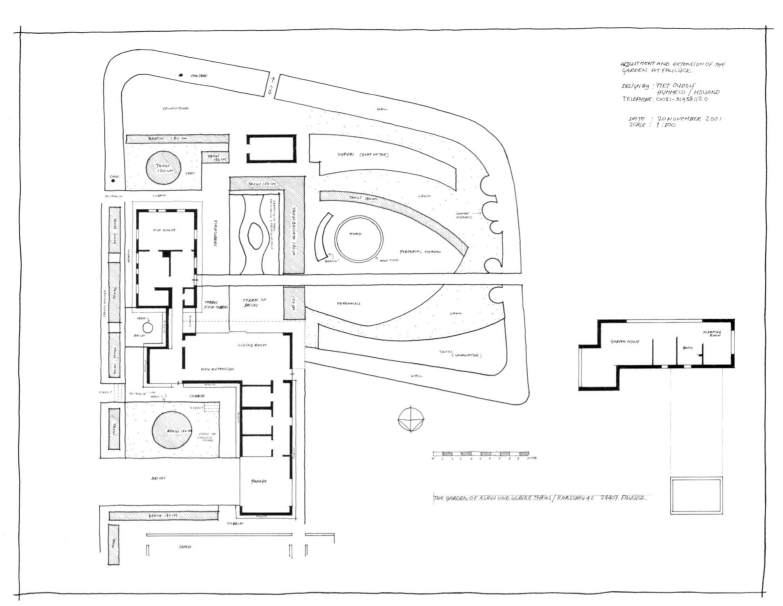

**Fagus sylvatica**

**Lawn**

**Taxus baccata**

# 2,000 m²

The prestigious Venice Biennale art exhibition, founded in 1895, has spawned subsidiary festivals over time—one of which is dedicated to architecture. Piet Oudolf was selected to make a garden that would embellish the grounds for the 2010 celebration, designed in conjunction with Japanese architect Kazuyo Sejima, principal of the Pritzker Prize–winning firm SANAA, who was named director of the Architecture Biennale for that year. The garden is planned to remain open throughout the following International Art Exhibition.

Venice, despite its dense urban fabric, has always been famous for the enclosed gardens of its wealthier citizens. The Oudolf garden is of course a public space but is placed so as to be "discovered" between the remains of the historic shipyards and naval depots that once served to provision and arm La Serenissima. Some existing plane trees, frequently used in European city squares, emphasize the public nature of the space, but the use of perennials and grasses creates a feeling of wilderness that echoes this dockyard area's long history of abandonment. Brambles on the perimeter of the plantings have been left as a visual cue to establish this link. The intended illusion is that of stepping into a tall meadow—an idealized version of nature.

The planting plan was conceived in two layers: groupings of single varieties of perennials and grasses, and an area of scattered structural plants intended to generate a naturalistic look through repetition. An important role is played by the grass *Molinia caerulea* 'Transparent,' which makes a dreamlike haze of flower and seedheads, and the flowering perennials *Eupatorium maculatum* and varieties of *Anemone x hybrida*. There is an emphasis on late summer and autumn color and texture. Many of the perennials and grasses will also remain attractive through the winter, even in an advanced state of decay. A central lawn and seats on the main path through the plantings are designed to be used for contemplation and relaxation. Temporary summer blooming plants are included—a rarity in Oudolf gardens—such as varieties of dahlia, *Nicotiana sylvestris*, and the annual *Ammi majus*, whose umbellate cream flowers smooth the contrasts between competing colors and forms, as well as evoke wild places.

Vergini, Venice, Italy, 2010

# 2,000 m²

The prestigious Venice Biennale art exhibition, founded in 1895, has spawned subsidiary festivals over time—one of which is dedicated to architecture. Piet Oudolf was selected to make a garden that would embellish the grounds for the 2010 celebration, designed in conjunction with Japanese architect Kazuyo Sejima, principal of the Pritzker Prize–winning firm SANAA, who was named director of the Architecture Biennale for that year. The garden is planned to remain open throughout the following International Art Exhibition.

Venice, despite its dense urban fabric, has always been famous for the enclosed gardens of its wealthier citizens. The Oudolf garden is of course a public space but is placed so as to be "discovered" between the remains of the historic shipyards and naval depots that once served to provision and arm La Serenissima. Some existing plane trees, frequently used in European city squares, emphasize the public nature of the space, but the use of perennials and grasses creates a feeling of wilderness that echoes this dockyard area's long history of abandonment. Brambles on the perimeter of the plantings have been left as a visual cue to establish this link. The intended illusion is that of stepping into a tall meadow—an idealized version of nature.

The planting plan was conceived in two layers: groupings of single varieties of perennials and grasses, and an area of scattered structural plants intended to generate a naturalistic look through repetition. An important role is played by the grass *Molinia caerulea* 'Transparent,' which makes a dreamlike haze of flower and seedheads, and the flowering perennials *Eupatorium maculatum* and varieties of *Anemone x hybrida*. There is an emphasis on late summer and autumn color and texture. Many of the perennials and grasses will also remain attractive through the winter, even in an advanced state of decay. A central lawn and seats on the main path through the plantings are designed to be used for contemplation and relaxation. Temporary summer blooming plants are included—a rarity in Oudolf gardens—such as varieties of dahlia, *Nicotiana sylvestris*, and the annual *Ammi majus*, whose umbellate cream flowers smooth the contrasts between competing colors and forms, as well as evoke wild places.

Il Giardino delle Vergini, Venice, Italy, 2010

IL GIARDINO DELLE VERGINI
THE ARSENAL, VENICE

GARDEN AND PLANTING DESIGN (PLAN)
PIET OUDOLF 2010

WALKING AND SITTING AREA

TOWER

TANK

DEPOT

PJE

PJE

TREE

GRASS AREA

GRASS LAWN

GRASS AREA

1:100

# 2,000 m²

Oudolf's first commission in Britain was here, in Surrey, though he had been visiting it for many years, buying plants from nurseries and getting to know their owners and plantsman-gardeners. The British people who had heard of Oudolf in the 1990s therefore thought of him as a nurseryman who grew interesting plants and, as a kind of sideline, designed gardens. In fact, this was the opposite of the real situation: Oudolf and his wife, Anja, had set up a nursery in order to grow plants for his design business. John Coke, the owner of Bury Court, had known Oudolf for some years—he too had a nursery business, Green Farm Plants, well known among plant aficionados for new introductions and rarities.

When Coke took possession of Bury Court, it was an abandoned farmyard with buildings of traditional flint and brick. The central area was largely hard surface, which had to be broken up and replaced with quality soil before any gardening could begin. High walls were also constructed to link the house with other buildings. Oudolf's design is dominated by a diagonal path that sweeps confidently across the former yard toward the only area that is not enclosed by walls.

There are borders of perennials, of course. For many, it was the first time they had seen Oudolf's dark color combinations: bronze foliage and mysterious deep-red flowers—in early summer. A still-greater innovation was the creation of a gravel garden, a genre almost unknown in Holland. Mediterranean plants had always been a particular love of Coke's, so it was a must that the new garden include some. Such plants play quite an important role in the drier gardens of southeast England, though for Oudolf this meant working with some species whose form was extremely removed from his normal range.

The courtyard contains several formally clipped shrubs as a foil to the perennials, including a circular metal structure that serves to train a dogwood hedge and a box sphere surrounded by a semicircle of the grass *Molinia caerulea*, emphasizing the place where the main path makes a bend. The garden's most radical and influential element is the Deschampsia Meadow, a 150-square-meter bed of one grass species (*Deschampsia cespitosa*) whose flower/seed heads create a hazy, misty effect from July until winter. Over the years, a number of different perennials have been introduced as contrasting elements to produce a carefully rationed flower or seedhead interest: the narrow spires of foxglove relative *Digitalis ferruginea* have been one, the deep-purple bobbles of *Allium sphaerocephalon* another. Since then this stylized meadow look and combination, along with other dark blends, has become quite fashionable with British gardeners.

Bury Court, Surrey, England, 1996

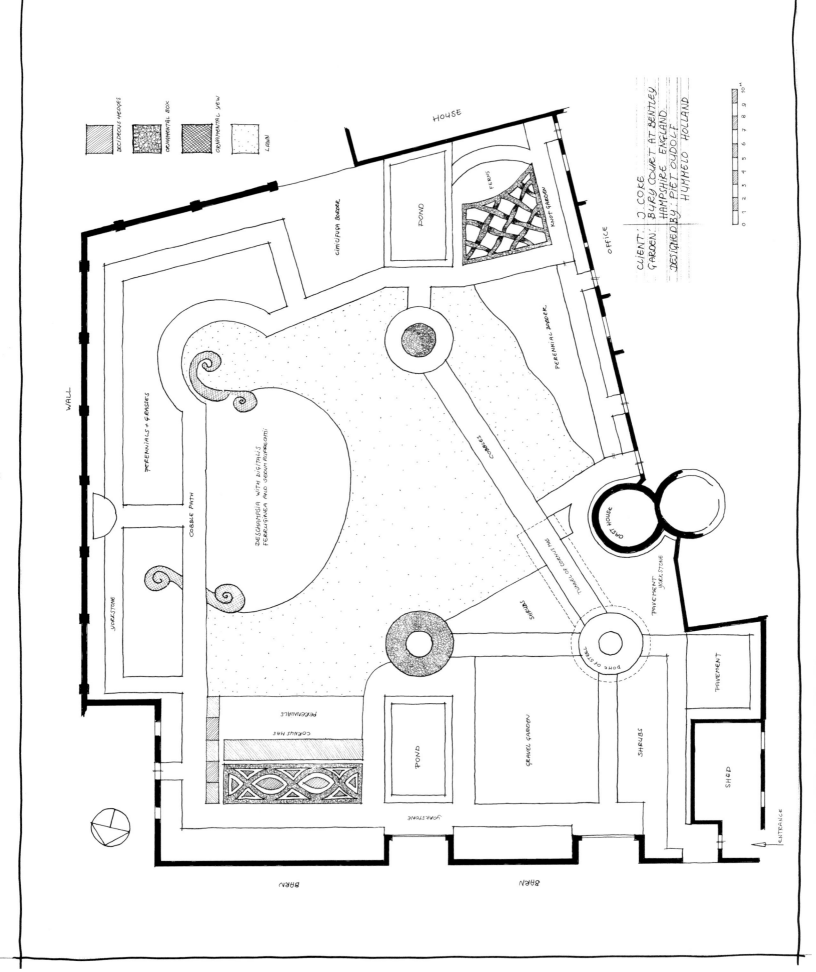

HOUSE

CLIENT : J. COKE
GARDEN : BURY COURT AT BENTLEY
HAMPSHIRE ENGLAND
DESIGNED BY : PIET OUDOLF
HUMMELO HOLLAND

0 1 2 3 4 5 6 7 8 9 10 M

DECIDUOUS HEDGES
ORNAMENTAL BOX
ORNAMENTAL YEW
LAWN

FERNS

POND

CIMICIFUGA BORDER

KNOT GARDEN

OFFICE

PERENNIAL BORDER

CORBLES

OAST HOUSE

PERENNIALS + GRASSES

WALL

COBBLE PATH

DESCHAMPSIA WITH DIGITALIS
FERRUGINEA AND SEDUM RUPRECHTII

TUNNEL OF CORNUS MAS

SHRUBS

PAVEMENT
YORKSTONE

YORKSTONE

DOME OF STEEL

PERENNIALS

CORNUS MAS

POND

GRAVEL GARDEN

SHRUBS

PAVEMENT

SHED

YORKSTONE

ENTRANCE

BARN

BARN

32

# 2,500 m²

Over the years, Piet Oudolf has created several gardens for houses by Piet Boon. The first, however, was for the architect himself. "He gave me complete freedom," he says, "but I wanted to follow his style of architecture, which is very strong, very personal—bold, modern, but with its Dutch roots clearly visible." Fertile humus-rich soil and a high water table made this site ideal for perennials, if somewhat more limiting for woody plants.

The 2,500-square-meter garden is dominated by one species, a grass, *Deschampsia cespitosa* 'Goldtau,' two great beds of which line the sides of a long, narrow swimming pool at the back of the house. Swimming pools are notoriously difficult to place in gardens, and countless designers have employed much effort and skill in hiding them. Oudolf's approach is an example of innovative lateral thinking—making the swimming pool the central feature instead.

*Deschampsia cespitosa* is a common native of northern Europe and characteristically grows in poor, wet soils. It flowers during July and August, producing masses of fine flower heads of palest green, which ripen to golden-yellow seedheads that last until December. These seedheads create a spectacular haze that seems like a romantic encapsulation of a wild meadow, luminescent with golden light but so vague in texture that the effect is almost dreamlike. From midwinter on, the seedheads disintegrate. They are cut back at the end of January, leaving behind neat tussocks of foliage featuring an attractive stripe as dark-green new leaves emerge to coexist with old leaves the color of sun-bleached straw. In spring, all becomes green again. Using an ornamental grass in this way makes the garden unmistakably contemporary, yet also links it to the Dutch landscape—both are orderly, with strong linear elements, and lush. The fertility of both is obvious for all to see. Wildness is present, albeit carefully controlled.

Running parallel to the grass and the yew hedges on either side are some borders of perennials: cultivars of the big ornamental grass *Miscanthus sinensis* are combined with the pink-flowered *Eupatorium maculatum* 'Atropurpureum,' both of which are about 2 meters high; yellow-, red-, and tan-colored helenium hybrids; and the scarlet "tails" of *Persicaria amplexicaulis*. These are grown intermingled together.

This garden shows that the New Naturalism of perennial planting is a style that can incorporate not only plenty of variety but real discipline too, and that ornamental grasses in particular do not have to be associated with a loose or antigeometrical aesthetic. It also demonstrates how a very humble plant can be plucked from obscurity and used to great effect.

Boon Garden, Oostzaan, The Netherlands, 2000

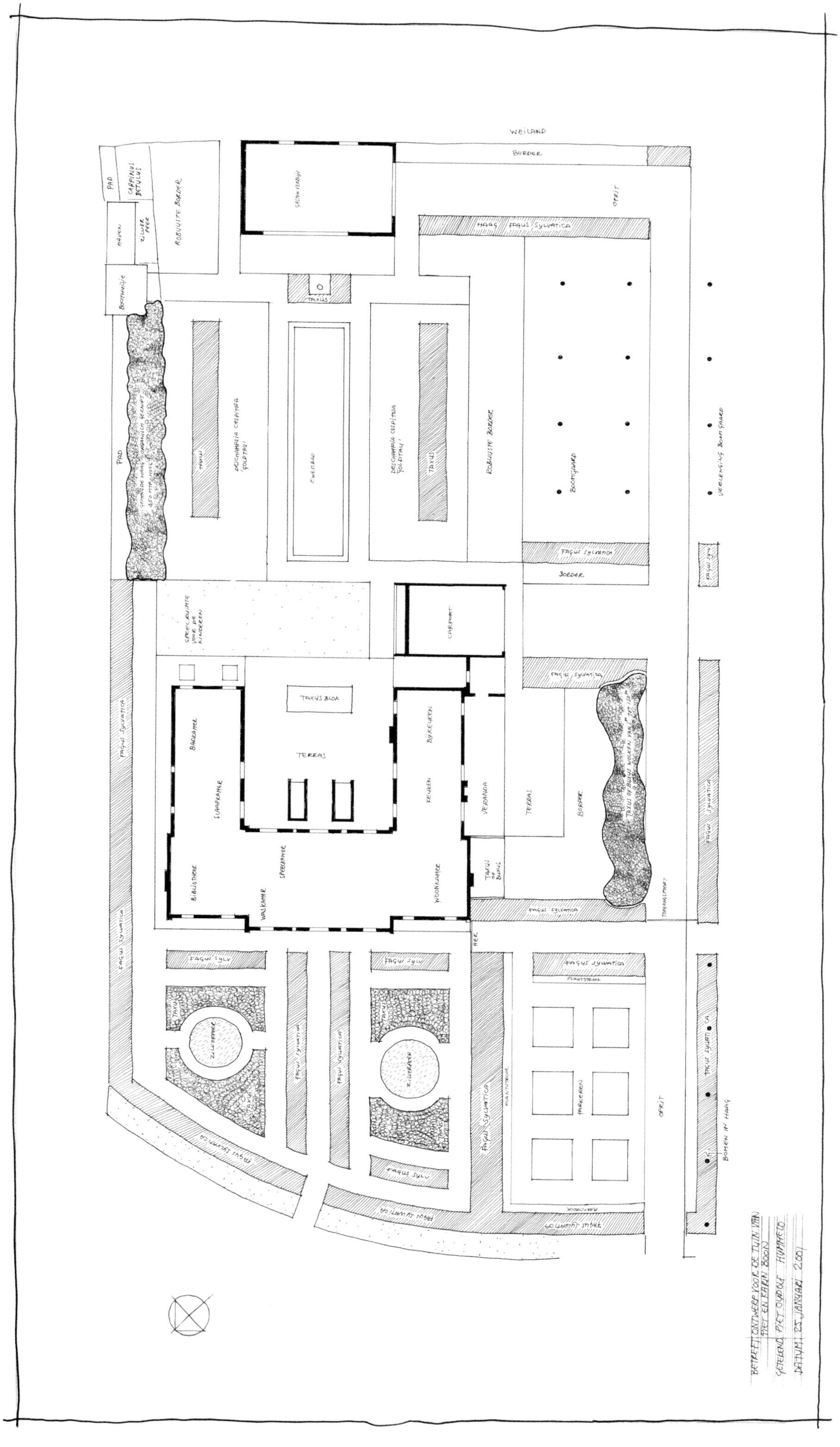

WEILAND

BORDER

HAAG FAGUS SYLVATICA

OPRIT

FAGUS SYLVATICA
BORDER

TERRAS

TAXUSBLOK

FAGUS SYLVATICA

BOMEN IN HAAG

BETREFT: ONTWERP VOOR DE TUIN VAN
HET EHEPAAR BOON
TEKENING: PRE-ONTWERP THOMATO
DATUM: 25 JANUARI 2001

# 2,500 m²

Potters Fields Park, on the south bank of the Thames in the heart of London—with its views of Tower Bridge, the Tower of London, and now the contemporary glass bubble of Foster + Partners' City Hall—has been one of the city's most iconic and visited sites for generations. Potters Field was originally a cemetery for unidentified or impoverished people; some gravestones, for the people lucky enough to have them, can still be seen near the Tooley Street entrance. Landscape architecture firm Gross Max was hired by the Greater London Authority to redevelop this public park and make it suitable for both private enjoyment and public cultural events. The company asked Oudolf to design a planting scheme with a genuinely distinctive look.

Once this area was known for its production of a version of Dutch Delftware pottery, making current Dutch involvement all the more appropriate. A sculpture evokes that history with leafy metal tendrils that recall the patterns of the glaze used on the ceramics. Eelco Hooftman, the founder of Gross Max, explains that the aim was to "bring landscape and nature into the city, to experience nature in the contemporary." On bringing Oudolf into the project, he explains that, "we wanted him to develop a new, romantic look . . . With him we have an affinity. We hardly need to talk." Hooftman describes the garden as deriving from the tradition of the *hortus conclusus*, or secret garden, an intensely sensual place that is "as much about planting as about space."

The development of the 1.5-hectare park involved "endless meetings with people locally," recalls Hooftman. "The whole process was very democratic." Establishing a trust to manage the park, something the group accomplished, however, was also fundamental to its long-term future success. That was "our biggest achievement," he says. "To take it out of the hands of the councils and put it into the hands of a trust enables us to have a head gardener." The future of the planting here will now be in sympathetic hands.

The planting consists of a series of stripes arranged in a jagged, dynamic way, each no more than a few meters wide. Individual stripes are a mixture of visually and culturally compatible plant varieties that harmonize with their adjacent stripes. Paths and walkways bisect the plantings, allowing visitors an up-close view of each.

Potters Fields Park, London, England, 2007

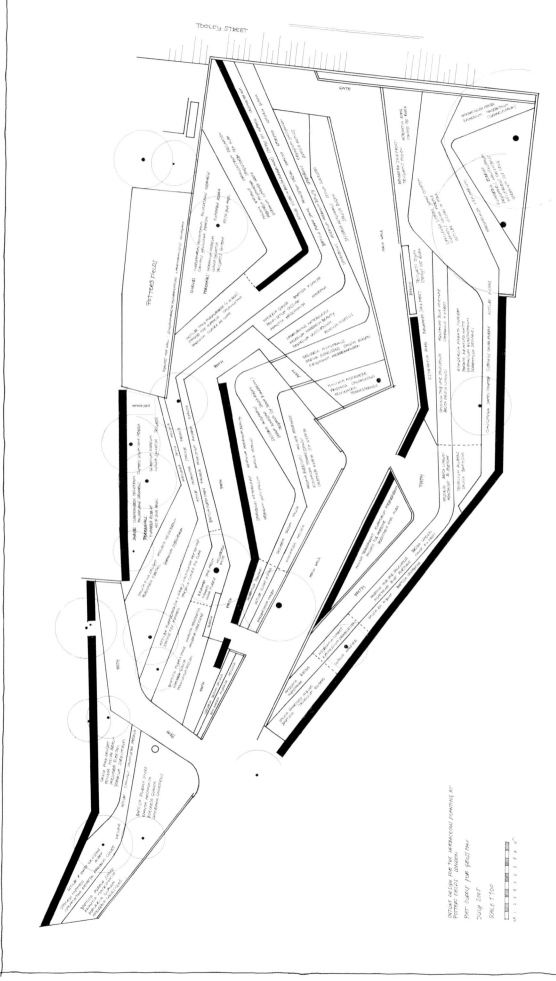

45

# 3,000 m²

The transformation of the once-industrial city of Essen, in Germany's Ruhrgebiet, into a "European Capital of Culture" may seem like an unachievable feat to those who are familiar with its past. This highly sought-after European Union designation is bestowed upon just a few cities each year, with the intent to stimulate postindustrial change in places that would benefit most from the socioeconomic impact and cultural development it was designed to bring. This influx of development can extend beyond a city's borders and into the surrounding area as well, and for Essen, this includes the Ebel district in Bottrop-Süd, where a new public park is being developed by landscape architecture firm Davids Terfrüchte + Partner on a former industrial site. With many seasonal events and festivals taking place in Germany, the government has committed to developing a component of each that will last beyond the function's end and permanently enrich the space. The country's famous summer-long garden shows, for example, are designed and sited in ways that will promote permanent regeneration of problem areas.

Here two concrete tanks originally built for industrial water treatment are being planted as an art installation. One of the 72-meter-wide tanks will be a repurposed water garden; the other is slated to become a sunken perennial garden designed by Oudolf and landscape architecture firm Gross Max. This planting is an example of the latest manifestation of the "layered" approach to planting he has been experimenting with for years.

A matrix, island, and scatter form three distinct visual layers. A path follows a spiral route around a series of concentric circles of planting. Each circular zone comprises a matrix planting of ground-covering, relatively low-growing plants in an intermingled blend. Within this are "island plants" where irregularly shaped beds are planted with a mixture of grasses for a late-summer-to-winter period of interest. Then there are scatter plants, taller species, often colorful or with distinct structure. These are clearly arranged throughout the matrix mix, but in distinct wavelike groups rather than at random. The groups of island plants and the scatter plants include varieties common to different parts of the circular matrix. They provide a rhythm that is the same throughout, while the matrix is like a melody that changes as one moves throughout the space. The layering technique is not only about aesthetics but also about making highly complex plantings easier to achieve—each can be set out separately, in turn.

Berne Park, Bottrop, Germany, 2010

| Area | Plant Name | % | Number of Plants |
|---|---|---|---|
| A¹ | *Scatter plants* | | |
| | Amsonia hubrichtii | | 8 |
| | Aster 'Oktoberlicht' | | 5 |
| | Baptisia leucantha | | 3 |
| | Festuca mairei | | 1 |
| | Pycnanthemum muticum | | 15 |
| | *Island plants* | | |
| | Deschampsia cespitosa 'Goldtau' | | 26 |
| | *Matrix planting* | | |
| | Sedum 'Matrona' | 35% | 131 |
| | Sesleria autumnalis | 25% | 94 |
| | Stachys officinalis 'Hummelo' | 40% | 150 |
| A² | *Scatter plants* | | |
| | Amsonia hubrichtii | | 16 |
| | Baptisia leucantha | | 15 |
| | Festuca mairei | | 9 |
| | Geranium psilostemon | | 9 |
| | Pycnanthemum muticum | | 57 |
| | *Island plants* | | |
| | Deschampsia cespitosa 'Goldtau' | | 277 |
| | Molinia 'Moorhexe' | | 274 |
| | *Matrix planting* | | |
| | Sedum 'Matrona' | 35% | 849 |
| | Sesleria autumnalis | 25% | 606 |
| | Stachys officinalis 'Hummelo' | 40% | 970 |
| B¹ | *Scatter plants* | | |
| | Amsonia hubrichtii | | 16 |
| | Aster 'Oktoberlicht' | | 11 |
| | Baptisia leucantha | | 12 |
| | Festuca mairei | | 4 |
| | Geranium psilostemon | | 9 |
| | Pycnanthemum muticum | | 105 |
| | *Island plants* | | |
| | Deschampsia cespitosa 'Goldtau' | | 201 |
| | Molinia 'Moorhexe' | | 183 |
| | *Matrix planting* | | |
| | Limonium latifolium | 20% | 356 |
| | Salvia 'Purple Rain' | 35% | 622 |
| | Stachys officinalis 'Hummelo' | 45% | 800 |
| B² | *Scatter plants* | | |
| | Amsonia hubrichtii | | 20 |
| | Aster 'Oktoberlicht' | | 8 |
| | Baptisia leucantha | | 12 |
| | Festuca mairei | | 1 |
| | Geranium psilostemon | | 12 |
| | Pycnanthemum muticum | | 36 |
| | *Island plants* | | |
| | Deschampsia cespitosa 'Goldtau' | | 138 |
| | Molinia 'Moorhexe' | | 311 |
| | *Matrix planting* | | |
| | Limonium latifolium | 20% | 272 |
| | Salvia 'Purple Rain' | 35% | 476 |
| | Stachys officinalis 'Hummelo' | 45% | 612 |
| C | *Scatter plants* | | |
| | Amsonia hubrichtii | | 41 |
| | Aster 'Oktoberlicht' | | 11 |
| | Baptisia leucantha | | 30 |
| | Festuca mairei | | 3 |
| | Geranium psilostemon | | 6 |
| | Pycnanthemum muticum | | 153 |
| | *Island plants* | | |
| | Deschampsia cespitosa 'Goldtau' | | 233 |
| | Molinia 'Moorhexe' | | 577 |
| | *Matrix planting* | | |
| | Achillea 'Hella Glashoff' | 35% | 1393 |
| | Scabiosa japonica var. alpina | 25% | 995 |
| | Stachys officinalis 'Hummelo' | 40% | 1238 |

| Area | Plant Name | % | Number of Plants |
|---|---|---|---|
| D | *Scatter plants* | | |
| | Amsonia hubrichtii | | 27 |
| | Aster 'Oktoberlicht' | | 18 |
| | Baptisia leucantha | | 18 |
| | Festuca mairei | | 4 |
| | Geranium psilostemon | | 12 |
| | Pycnanthemum muticum | | 153 |
| | *Island plants* | | |
| | Deschampsia cespitosa 'Goldtau' | | 266 |
| | Molinia 'Moorhexe' | | 497 |
| | *Matrix planting* | | |
| | Calamintha nepeta ssp. nepeta | 20% | 873 |
| | Sedum 'Sunkissed' | 35% | 973 |
| | Stachys officinalis 'Hummelo' | 45% | 1251 |
| E | *Scatter plants* | | |
| | Aruncus 'Horatio' | | 151 |
| | Molinia 'Transparent' | | 96 |
| | Streams | | |
| | Salvia 'Pink Delight' | 30% | 428 |
| | Persicaria ampl. 'Alba' | 70% | 587 |
| | *Matrix planting* | | |
| | Persicaria ampl. 'Alba' | 35% | 1171 |
| | Deschampsia 'Goldtau' | 35% | 1171 |
| | Anemone 'Pamina' | 30% | 1359 |
| | Plant total | | 21,467 |

Plants set out in the following order:

1. All individual big groups: Molinia, Deschampsia

2. Scatter plants including Stachys 'Hummelo'

3. Filler plants
   Bed A1, A2
   Sedum and Sesleria in groups of 9 and 11

   Bed B1, B2
   Salvia in groups of 9
   Limonium in groups of 3

   Bed C
   Scabiosa in groups of 5
   Achillea in groups of 12 and 15

   Bed D
   Sedum in groups of 9 and 12
   Calamintha in groups of 5

   Bed E
   Set out Deschampsia in groups of 3 or 5 and fill in with Persicaria
   Streams: Salvia in groups of 5 to 7 and fill in with Persicaria

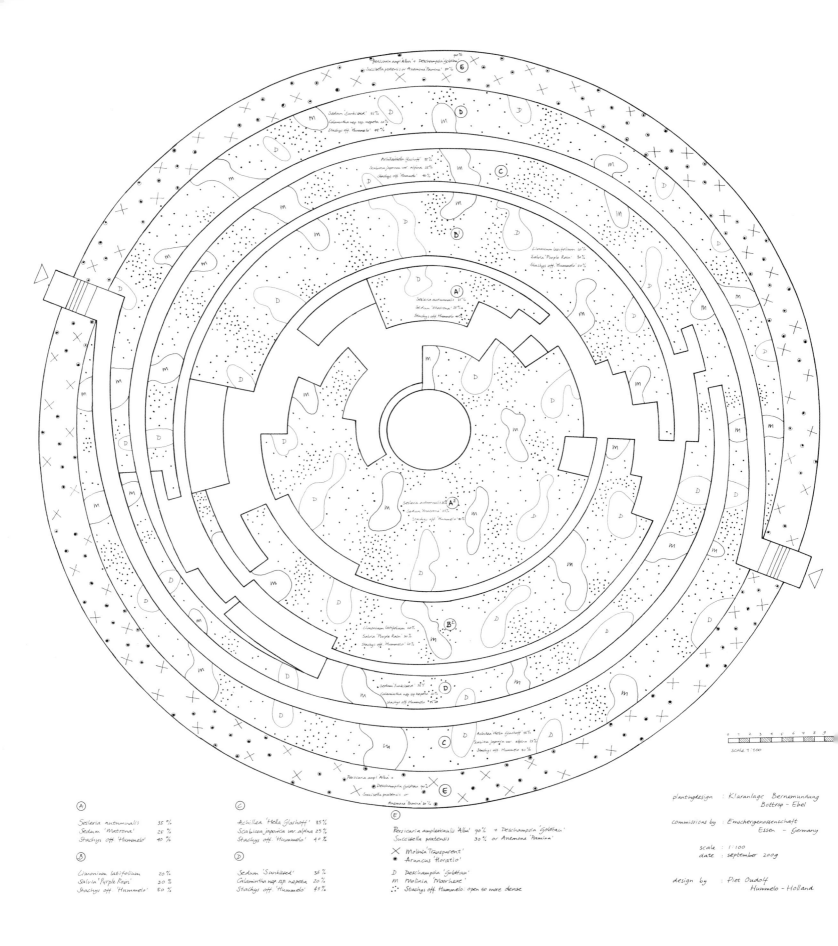

Scale 1:100

planting design : Klaranlage  Bernemundung
                                Bottrop - Ebel

commissions by : Emschergenossenschaft
                                Essen - Germany

scale : 1:100
date : september 2009

design by : Piet Oudolf
                        Hummelo - Holland

Ⓐ

Sesleria autumnalis        35 %
Sedum 'Matrona'            25 %
Stachys off. 'Hummelo'    40 %

Ⓑ

Limonium latifolium        20 %
Salvia 'Purple Rain'        30 %
Stachys off. 'Hummelo'    50 %

Ⓒ

Achillea 'Hela Glashoff'          35 %
Scabiosa japonica var. alpina 25 %
Stachys off. 'Hummelo'            40 %

Ⓓ

Sedum 'Sunkissed'                      35 %
Calamintha nep. ssp nepeta        20 %
Stachys off. 'Hummelo'                45 %

Ⓔ

Persicaria amplexicaulis 'Alba' 90%  + Deschampsia 'Goldtau'
Succisella pratensis              30 % or Anemone 'Pamina'

✕  Molinia 'Transparent'
⊙  Aruncus 'Horatio'

Ⓓ  Deschampsia 'Goldtau'
Ⓜ  Molinia 'Moorhexe'
∴  Stachys off. Hummelo: open to more dense

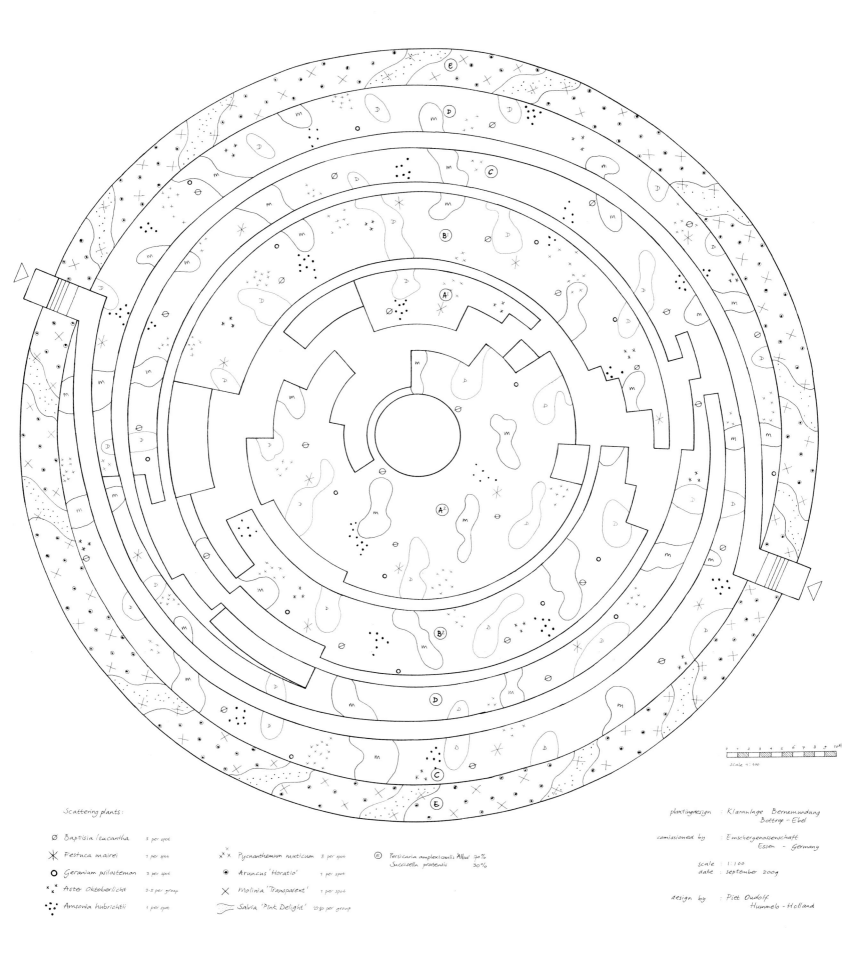

Scattering plants:

Ø  *Baptisia leucantha*     3 per spot

✳  *Festuca mairei*     1 per spot

○  *Geranium psilostemon*     3 per spot

✢  *Aster Oktoberlicht*     3-5 per group

⋮  *Amsonia hubrichtii*     1 per spot

ˣ✗  *Pycnanthemum muticum*     3 per spot

◉  *Aruncus 'Horatio'*     1 per spot

✕  *Molinia 'Transparent'*     1 per spot

〜  *Salvia 'Pink Delight'*     25-30 per group

Ⓔ  *Persicaria amplexicaulis 'Alba'* 70%
   *Succisella pratensis*         30%

Scale 1:100

plantingdesign : Klaranlage  Bernemundung
                 Bottrop - Ebel

comissioned by : Emschergenossenschaft
                 Essen  - Germany

scale : 1:100
date : september 2009

design by : Piet Oudolf
            Hummelo - Holland

# 3,000 m²

This house, renovated by architect Piet Boon, is situated within the curve of one of Rotterdam's canals. The site's woodland trees make a fine backdrop for a garden whose own mature trees reveal that it must have been created in the early twentieth century. The presence of a swamp cypress (*Taxodium distichum*) also discloses that the water table must be high.

Oudolf's plan called for the development of a number of new, discrete areas in the 3,000-square-meter garden, which was previously dominated by a vast lawn. Now the main elements are a terrace with a swimming pool surrounded by decking and two beds of perennial planting. A border of large, colorful perennials runs along one side of the terrace. With the surrounding woodland behind it, the transition between the two becomes seamless: the perennials appear as the edge of the woodland itself. Yet this is not a particularly naturalistic planting. The clumps of heleniums, *Persicaria amplexicaulis*, and molinia and miscanthus grasses, which flower from midsummer to midautumn, are colorful and familiar enough to be read as a relatively conventional border and an exuberant addition to a swimming area. On the other side of the pool is a narrower border, which is open to the remaining sweep of lawn on the rear. Here a number of interesting small trees coexist with a rich underplanting of perennials that will tolerate light shade as the trees develop, including *Geranium* 'Cambridge' and *Anemone hupehensis* var. *japonica* 'Pamina.'

Between the swimming pool and the house is an 18-meter-long hedge cut in the "regularly irregular" version of cloud pruning that is signature Oudolf. To either side, grass *Sesleria autumnalis* is interspersed with lower-growing varieties of *Sedum*. At the front of the house are several hedges of box, a simple, almost minimalist statement.

Witteveen Garden, Rotterdam, The Netherlands, 2005

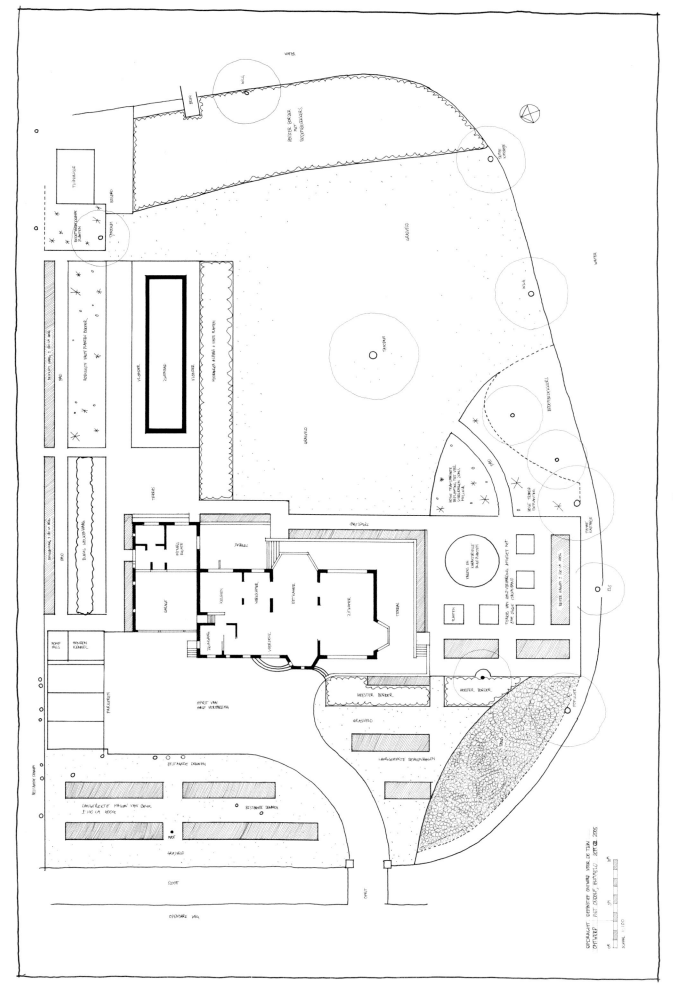

59

# 3,400 m²

When the British Royal Horticultural Society commissioned Oudolf to design a new double border in its garden in Woking, Surrey, just outside London, the society probably had in mind a more naturalistic and contemporary version of the vast double border that had long been a feature of the garden. What it received, however, was something considerably more radical, almost experimental. In the design, Oudolf began to develop a very sophisticated new approach to planting that creates blends of several plants and then uses the blends in nuanced variations throughout the length of the border.

Initial reactions to this new border were mixed, but to be fair, it was installed long before the construction of the new greenhouse, which now sits at the bottom of the slope. It also includes a deciduous shrubby backdrop that does much to provide a framework and direct the gaze down the length of the border toward the greenhouse, very much the jewel in the crown of the Wisley garden—but of course this took time to grow. Problems with dry soil and the popularity of the border with the local rabbit community also affected many people's perceptions of the project in its first few years.

Now that those early problems have been overcome, the border can be fully appreciated as a genuinely new take on what had become tired and expected. The formally shaped Edwardian double border has been reworked for the twenty-first century. It is 150 meters long with two 12-meter-wide sections, on either side of a central 6-meter-wide grass path. The border is divided into 66 diagonal bands, 33 per side, the geometry of which disappears quickly when viewed as a long, composed whole. In summer, this is a symphony of flower color, with subtle repetitions, rhythms, and subrhythms; structure is asserted in autumn when seedheads and fading foliage show every imaginable shade of fawn, brown, and yellow. For those unused to seeing "dead" plants used with aesthetic intent, the border in November or December can be revelatory.

Each band contains three or four perennial varieties and/or grasses. The plants combined within each band were chosen for their aesthetic relationships to each other—especially regarding height and foliage—and for their ability to provide interest over a large part of the season. No single band is ever repeated. Structural plants that dominate visually over longer distances tend to be used in lower proportions than plants that are less structural or that flower earlier. The bands work together to create a spread of seasonal interest and of color, structure, and texture. Much of the impact of the border comes from the way the viewer, often subconsciously, detects linkages between the same plant or the same partial combination of plants appearing in several areas of the field of vision.

This blending of perennial plants is a relatively new style of gardening, representing a clear break with the tradition of creating one-variety blocks. It is an approach that requires much research, because apart from aesthetic issues, maintenance must be carefully thought through, particularly regarding the different rates at which plants may grow and therefore compete with each other.

Wisley, Royal Horticultural Society Garden, Surrey, England, 2001

Rudbeckia maxima

Phlomis tuberosa

Eryngium yuccifolium

Perovskia 'Little Spire'

Echinacea pallida

Plant leaves

Plant Proportions

# 4,000 m²

Oudolf's first large-scale public commission came in the form of this park in central Sweden, which now totals 4,000 square meters. The town of Enköping is renowned for its creative use of horticulture in parks and small "pocket parks" that are intensely designed and planted. At a latitude of fifty-nine degrees north—not too far from the latitude of the southern tip of Greenland—it was a challenge to select suitable species. On the positive side, though, the summers can be warm, and many plants benefit from the famous Nordic sun when, for several weeks on either side of Midsummer's Day in June, it is never completely dark. Plant selection was crucial, so Oudolf relied heavily on the advice of Swedish colleagues, especially Stefan Mattson, the town parks director.

Those unfamiliar with Sweden might be astonished at the range of plants used or the fact that so many of them originate from much further south. In reality there are limitations, particularly on species that need warm nights or flower late in the growing season. For this reason, many North American prairie species could not be included: varieties of *Solidago* and *Vernonia* or any American grasses. Varieties of *Aster* and *Rudbeckia*, however, were judged tolerant enough. Some plants from the monsoon climates of eastern Asia, accustomed to hot and humid summers, such as *Anemone x hybrida*, have not flourished, and only a few *Miscanthus* varieties flower reliably. Among the grasses that have flourished are several species of *Achnatherum brachytricha* and varieties of *Molinia caerulea*.

At the time the Dream Park was created, Oudolf tended to favor the use of hedges as a way of creating architectural structure to contrast with the informality of the perennials. This use of traditional clipping techniques to create structural blocks was a very important theme in Holland's modernist garden movement. Here the blocks are created by three "towers," discontinuous circles of beech hedging forming enclosed areas. Oudolf also took the idea of monocultural blocks and extended it to perennials. Of course, using blocks of perennials is common, but Oudolf took the idea further than usual by selecting one variety—or very similar cultivars of one variety—to create a single dramatic feature, in this case the "Salvia River." Three cultivars are used: *Salvia nemorosa* 'Ostfriesland,' *S. x sylvestris* 'Blauhügel,' and 'Rügen.' All are of similar height and flower in early summer. "It was an experiment. It became a great success," he says. "I copied it for the Lurie Garden in Chicago." This approach has also now been emulated by garden designers elsewhere.

Dream Park, Enköping, Sweden, 1996 First phase 2003 Second phase

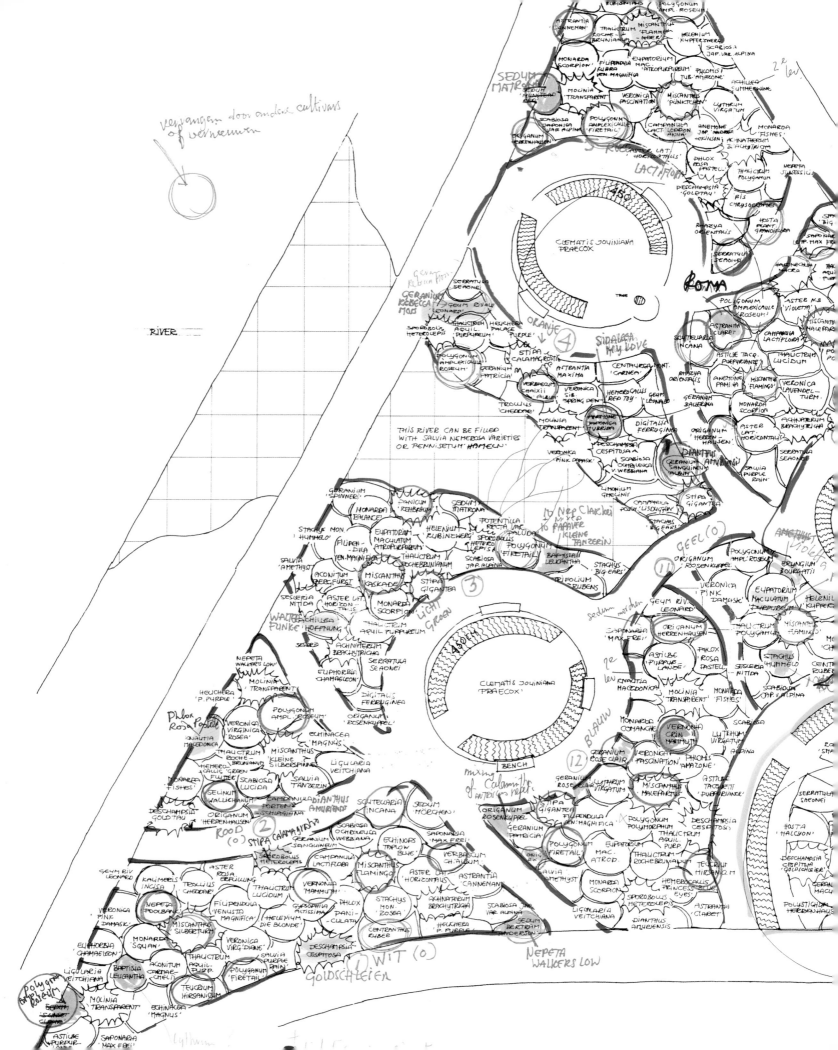

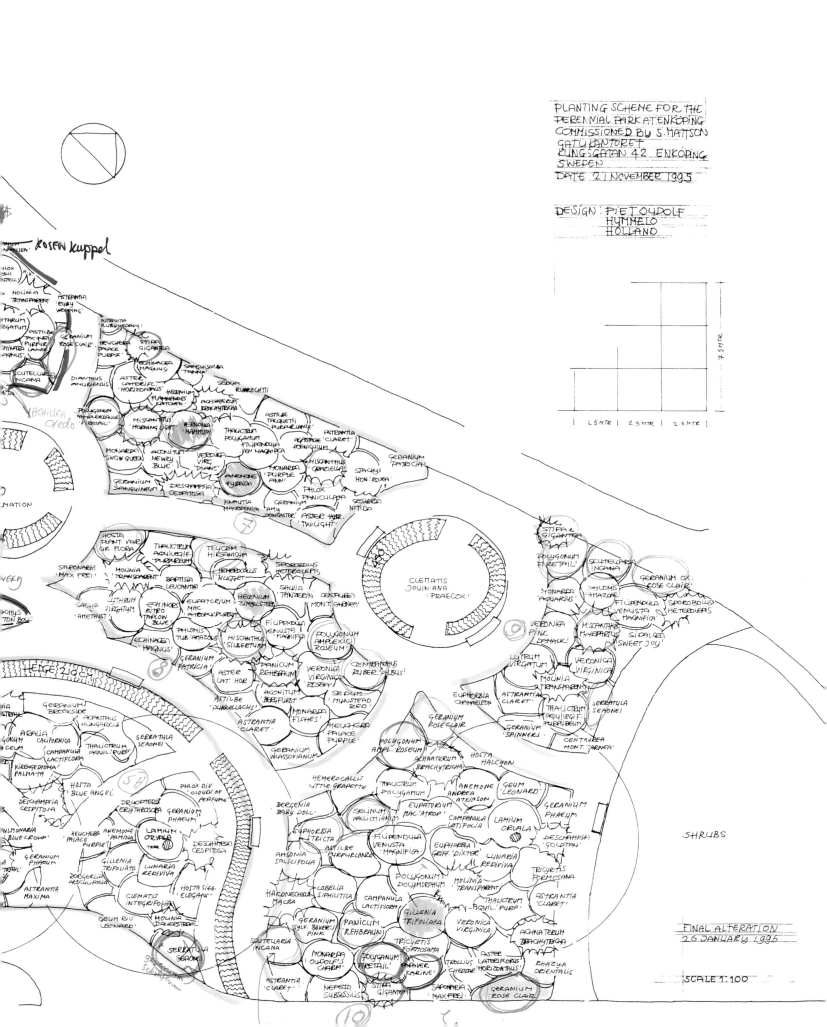

PLANTING SCHEME FOR THE
PERENNIAL PARK AT ENKÖPING
COMMISSIONED BY S. MATTSON
GATUKONTORET
KUNGSGATAN 42 ENKÖPING
SWEDEN
DATE 21 NOVEMBER 1995

DESIGN: PIET OUDOLF
        HUMMELO
        HOLLAND

ROSEN KUPPEL

CLEMATIS
JOUINIANA
'PRAECOX'

HEDGE 2.10 CM

SHRUBS

FINAL ALTERATION
26 JANUARY 1996

SCALE 1:100

7.5 MTR

2.5 MTR | 2.5 MTR | 2.5 MTR

# 4,500 m²

Bad Driburg is a spa town in the German state of North Rhine-Westphalia, with all the parks and elegant buildings typical of the European resort towns where people have gone for over two centuries to take the waters and receive health cures. Its main historic park, Gräflicher Park, can now add a contemporary garden designed by Oudolf to its list of amenities. "It was created as part of an arts project," he says. "It rather lacked contrast, so I had to make sure that it had plenty of atmosphere of its own." Essentially, broad paths run between two sets of double borders 10 to 14 meters wide. The width of the paths and the borders both vary slightly at different points to create a sense of flow and movement. The paved paths are interrupted at five points by circles of lawn grass although, unlike any conventional lawn, these are mounded and recessed at irregular intervals to further enhance the feel of wavelike motion. This is not only aesthetically pleasing but also serves the practical purpose of directing water after a rain, which is necessary to assist drainage on the heavy clay soil. Two of the areas work as "swales," bowls for temporary detention of water. A stand of *Magnolia x loebneri* 'Merrill' was included to help provide a visual background for the design.

The planting is intended to reach no more than 1.2 meters high and emphasizes colorful perennials with a long season. The design also aims for biodiversity, providing nectar for insects, food and shelter for invertebrates, and seed for birds. Cultivars of *Iris sibirica*, *Salvia*, *Astilbe*, *Achillea*, and *Nepeta* make an impact in early summer; later, cultivars of *Echinacea purpurea*, *Sedum*, *Aster*, *Lythrum*, and *Persicaria* take over, along with shorter grasses such as *Calamagrostis brachytricha* and *Molinia caerulea* 'Heidebraut.' Most of the planting is in clumps, but a few perennials are scattered to provide widely spread splashes of color that unify the whole. In early summer, *Papaver orientale* 'Mandarin' does this, with *Agastache* 'Blue Fortune' and *Monarda* 'Scorpion' later on. In late summer, the venerable Dutch *Helenium* 'Moerheim Beauty' performs this role. *Veronicastrum virginicum* 'Temptation' is also dotted. Its early-to-midsummer flowers turn to strong seedheads, providing continuity from early summer to midwinter.

Gräflicher Park, Bad Driburg, Germany, 2008

**Plant List by Bed**

**Bed 1**
Achillea 'Hella Glashoff'
Achillea 'Walter Funcke'
Amsonia tab. var. salicifolia
Anemone 'Honorine Jobert'
Aster 'Rosa Erfüllung'
Aster 'Sonora'
Astilbe 'Visions in Pink'
Echinacea 'Fatal Attraction'
Echinacea 'Rubinglow'
Geranium soboliferum
Iris sibirica 'Perry's Blue'
Knautia macedonica
Liatris spicata
Lythrum virgatum
Molinia 'Heidebraut'
Nepeta 'Walker's Low'
Pennisetum 'Cassian'
Perovskia 'Blue Spire'
Salvia 'Mainacht'
Sedum 'Matrona'
Sedum 'Red Cauli'
Sesleria nitida
Stachys off. 'Rosea'
Stachys off.'Hummelo'
Veronica spicata 'Rotfuchs'

**Bed 2**
Achillea 'Hella Glashoff'
Achillea 'Walter Funcke'
Amsonia tab. var. salicifolia
Anemone 'Honorine Jobert'
Aster 'Sonora'
Astilbe 'Visions in Pink'
Echinacea 'Fatal Attraction'
Echinacea 'Rubinglow'
Echinacea 'Virgin'
Geranium soboliferum
Iris sibirica 'Perry's Blue'
Knautia macedonica
Liatris spicata
Lythrum virgatum
Molinia 'Heidebraut'
Nepeta 'Walker's Low'
Pennisetum 'Cassian'
Perovskia 'Little Spire'
Salvia 'Mainacht'
Sedum 'Matrona'
Sesleria nitida
Stachys off. 'Hummelo'
Stachys off. 'Rosea'
Veronica spicata 'Rotfuchs'

**Bed 3**
Achillea 'Walter Funcke'
Achnatherum brachytricha
Amsonia tab. var. salicifolia
Anemone 'Pamina'
Aster amellus 'Rosa Erfüllung'
Astilbe 'Visions in Red'
Calamintha nep. ssp. nepeta
Echinacea 'Rocky Top'
Echinacea 'Rubinglow'
Echinacea 'Vintage Wine'
Eryngium yuccifolium
Geranium soboliferum
Helenium 'Rubinzwerg'
Iris sib.'Light Blue'
Iris sib.'Ruffled Velvet'
Knautia macedonica
Limonium latifolium
Lythrum 'Zigeunerblut'
Lythrum virgatum
Molinia 'Moorhexe'
Nepeta faassenii
Origanum 'Herrenhausen'
Panicum 'Shenandoah'
Pennisetum 'Woodside'
Penstemon digitalis
Perovskia 'Little Spire'
Persicaria 'Firedance'
Phlomis russeliana
Pycnanthemum muticum
Salvia 'Amethyst'

Salvia 'Tänzerin'
Salvia vert. 'Purple Rain'
Sedum 'Matrona'
Sedum 'Sunkissed'
Sesleria autumnalis
Sesleria caerulea
Sesleria nitida
Solidaster 'Lemore'
Sporobolus heterolepis
Stachys off. 'Rosea'
Stachys off. 'Hummelo'
Tradescantia 'Concord Grape'
Tradescantia 'Perinne's Pink'
Veronica 'Evelyn'

**Bed 4**
Achillea 'Hella Glashoff'
Achillea 'Walter Funcke'
Achnaterum brachytricha
Amsonia tab. var. salicifolia
Anemone 'Pamina'
Aster 'Rosa Erfüllung'
Aster 'Twilight'
Astilbe 'Visions in Red'
Echinacea 'Fatal Attraction'
Echinacea 'Green Edge'
Eryngium yuccifolium
Helenium 'Rubinzwerg'
Iris sib.'Light Blue'
Iris sib.'Ruffled Velvet'
Knautia macedonica
Limonium latifolium
Lythrum 'Zigeunerblut'
Lythrum virgatum
Molinia 'Moorhexe'
Nepeta faassenii
Origanum 'Herrenhausen'
Panicum 'Shenandoah'
Penstemon digitalis
Perovskia 'Little Spire'
Persicaria 'Firedance'
Phlomis russeliana
Pycnanthemum muticum
Salvia 'Amethyst'
Salvia 'Tänzerin'
Sedum 'Matrona'
Sedum 'Sunkissed'
Sesleria caerulea
Sesleria nitida
Solidaster 'Lemore'
Sporobolus heterolepis
Stachys off. 'Hummelo'
Tradescantia 'Concord Grape'
Tradescantia 'Perinne's Pink'
Tricyrtis formosana
Trifolium rubens
Veronica 'Eveline'

**Bed 5**
Achillea 'Walter Funcke'
Achnaterum brachytricha
Amsonia tab. var. salicifolia
Anemone 'Pamina'
Aster 'Sonora'
Aster 'Twilight'
Atilbe 'Visions in Red'
Calamintha nep. ssp. nepeta
Echinacea 'Rocky Top'
Echinacea 'Rubinglow'
Echinacea 'Vintage Wine'
Eryngium yuccifolium
Geranium soboliferum
Helenium 'Rubinzwerg'
Iris sib.'Blue Velvet'
Iris sib.'Light Blue'
Knautia macedonica
Liatris spicata
Limonium latifolium
Lythrum 'Zigeunerblut'
Lythrum virgatum
Molinia 'Moorhexe'
Nepeta faassenii
Panicum 'Shenandoah'
Pennisetum 'Woodside'
Penstemon digitalis
Perovskia 'Little Spire'

Persicaria 'Firedance'
Phlomis russeliana
Pycnanthemum muticum
Rhazya orientalis
Salvia 'Amethyst'
Salvia 'Purple Rain'
Salvia 'Tänzerin'
Sedum 'Matrona'
Sedum 'Sunkissed'
Sesleria autumnalis
Sesleria nitida
Sporobolus heterolepis
Stachys off. 'Hummelo'
Stachys off. 'Rosea'
Tradescantia 'Concord Grape'
Tricyrtis formosana
Trifolium rubens
Veronica 'Eveline'

**Bed 6**
Achillea 'Hella Glashoff'
Achnaterum brachytricha
Amsonia tab. var. salicifolia
Anemone 'Pamina'
Aster 'Rosa Erfüllung'
Aster 'Sonora'
Aster 'Twilight'
Astilbe 'Visions in Red'
Echinacea 'Rocky Top'
Echinacea 'Rubinglow'
Eryngium yuccifolium
Geranium soboliferum
Helenium 'Rubinzwerg'
Iris sib.'Blue Velvet'
Iris sib.'Light Blue'
Knautia macedonica
Liatris spicata
Limonium latifolium
Lythrum 'Zigeunerblut'
Lythrum virgatum
Molinia 'Moorhexe'
Nepeta faassenii
Panicum 'Shenandoah'
Pennisetum 'Woodside'
Penstemon digitalis
Perovskia 'Little Spire'
Persicaria 'Firedance'
Phlomis russeliana
Pycnanthemum muticum
Salvia 'Amethyst'
Salvia 'Purple Rain'
Salvia 'Tänzerin'
Sedum 'Sunkissed'
Sedum 'Matrona'
Sedum 'Sunkissed'
Sesleria autumnalis
Sesleria caerulea
Solidaster 'Lemore'
Sporobolus heterolepis
Stachys off. 'Hummelo'
Stachys off. 'Rosea'
Tradescantia 'Perinne's Pink'
Tricyrtis formosana
Trifolium rubens
Veronica 'Eveline'

**Individual Groups Scattered**

**Bed 1**
Helenium 'Moerheim Beauty'
Agastache 'Blue Fortune'
**Bed 2**
Helenium 'Moerheim Beauty'
Agastache 'Blue Fortune'
**Bed 3**
Monarda 'Scorpion'
Veronicastrum 'Temptation'
Papaver orientale 'Mandarin'
Agastache 'Blue Fortune'
**Bed 4**
Monarda 'Scorpion'
Veronicastrum 'Temptation'
Papaver orientale 'Mandarin'
Agastache 'Blue Fortune'
**Bed 5**
Monarda 'Scorpion'
Veronicastrum 'Temptation'
Papaver orientale 'Mandarin'
Agastache 'Blue Fortune'
**Bed 6**
Monarda 'Scorpion'
Veronicastrum 'Temptation'
Papaver orientale 'Mandarin'
Agastache 'Blue Fortune'

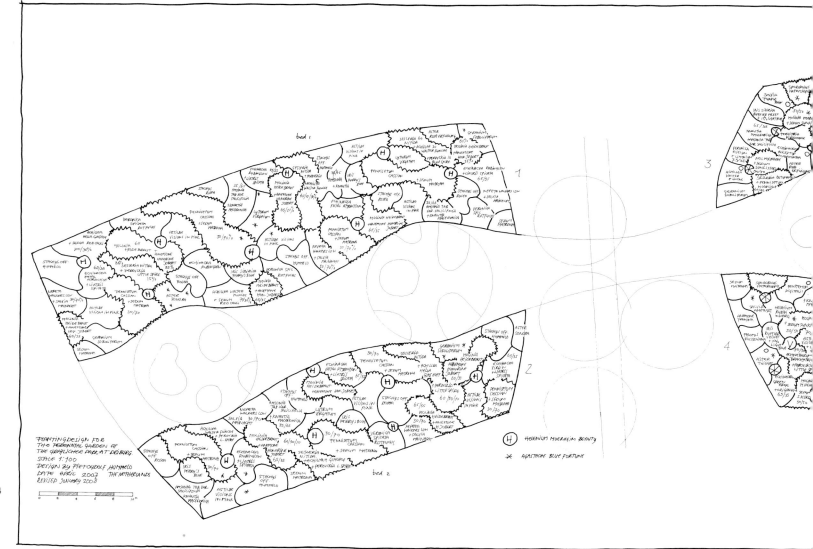

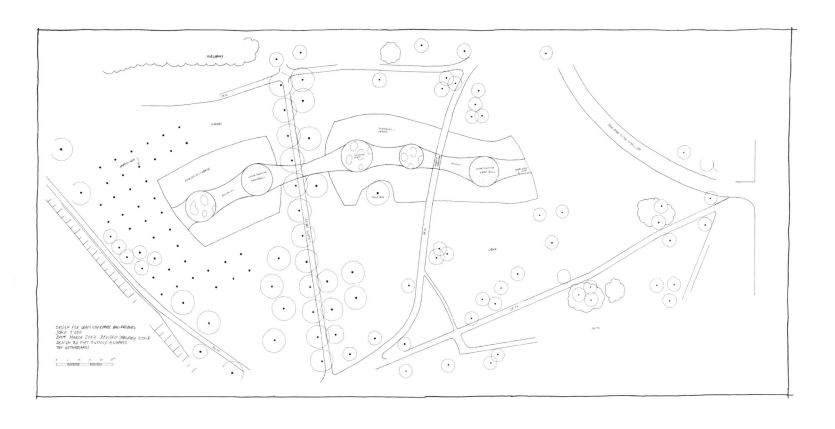

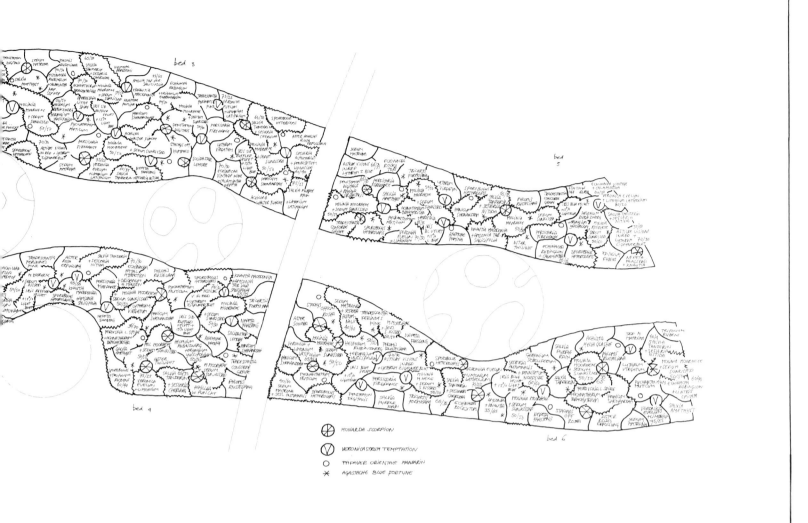

bed 3

bed 5

bed 4

bed 6

⊕ MONARDA SCORPION

Ⓥ VERONICASTRUM TEMPTATION

○ PAPAVER ORIENTALE MANDARIN

✳ AGASTACHE BLUE FORTUNE

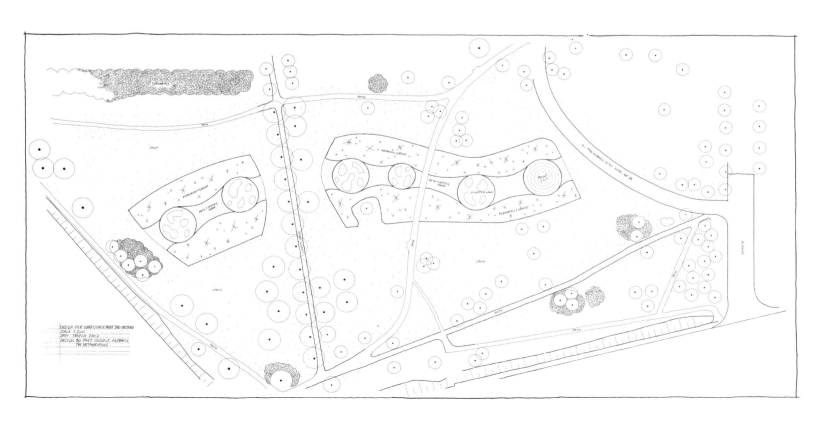

# 4,500 m²

Designed to serve as a visitor attraction commemorating the new millennium, this garden, Oudolf's second British commission, is located at the Pensthorpe Nature Reserve near Fakenham in Norfolk. The Pensthorpe trust's primary aim is to manage and encourage public access to a nature reserve with a variety of habitats: lakes, woodland, marsh, and grassland. But as with many similar institutions, the visitor attraction needed a whole portfolio of features to remain successful; here gardens with a wildlife or naturalistic theme supplement the key conservation areas. As well as Oudolf's garden, there is the Wildlife Habitat Garden and the Wave Garden designed by Julie Toll, a British garden designer famous for her wildflower-inspired projects. She is also a colleague of Oudolf's in the Perennial Perspectives movement, a broad, loose grouping of northern European garden and landscape designers.

Oudolf's modern, naturalistic planting was seen as an appropriate style for Pensthorpe to incorporate in hailing the new millennium. Unlike much of his previous work, this project did not involve relating to architecture; everything is quite informal. The landscape of Norfolk is famously flat and agricultural—indeed, Dutch engineers drained some areas in the eighteenth century to make the land arable. However, around Fakenham there is more elevation, and the design of the Millennium Garden benefits from gentle ups and downs and places where it is possible to see plants from slightly different levels. The soil is sandy, with some quite wet areas. Gates cross paths that take visitors out into the surrounding landscape, yet the textures and colors of the chosen grasses provide a continuity that leaps the fence.

Paths are broad to accommodate visitor numbers. They offer many different circuits and a variety of viewpoints across the 4,500 square meters of planting. For many who come, this is the first time they have seen perennials used on this scale, and the effect can be overwhelming, especially since the familiar markers of gardens—hedges, lawns, statuary, archways—are lacking. Visitors describe feeling like children in a meadow; their surroundings make them feel diminutive but full of wonder.

Spring sees flowering shrubs and bulbs, while summer builds to a crescendo of flowering perennials and grasses in early September. Late autumn and winter are dominated by grass seedheads, and it is around this time that the planting looks at its wildest and most natural. Birches and dogwoods with colored bark in the area near the perennials ensure that even in the depths of winter, there is something to enjoy.

**Pensthorpe Nature Reserve, Norfolk, England, 2000** Renovation 2008

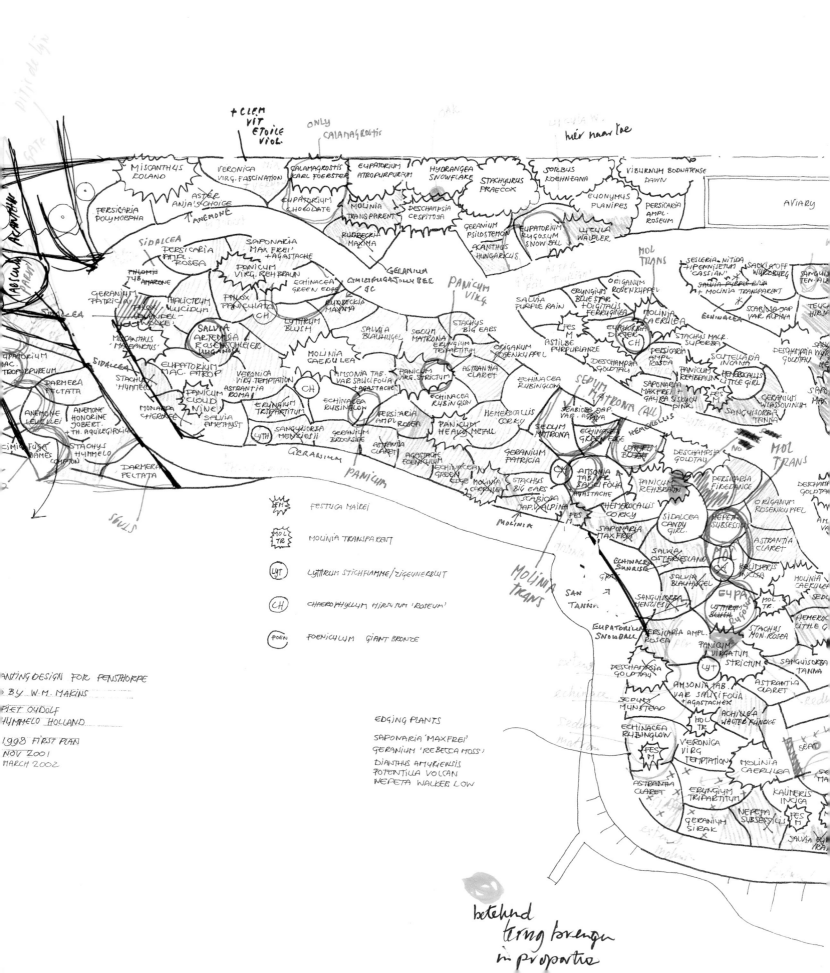

Planting design for Penshorpe by W.M. Makins. Piet Oudolf, Hummelo Holland. 1998 first plan. Nov 2001, March 2002.

Legend:
- FESTUCA MAIREI
- MOLINIA TRANSPARENT
- LYTHRUM STICHFLAMME/ZIGEUNERBLUT
- CHAEROPHYLLUM HIRSUTUM 'ROSEUM'
- FOENICULUM GIANT BRONZE

EDGING PLANTS:
- SAPONARIA 'MAXFREI'
- GERANIUM 'REBECCA MOSS'
- DIANTHUS AMURIENSIS
- POTENTILLA VOLCAN
- NEPETA WALKER LOW

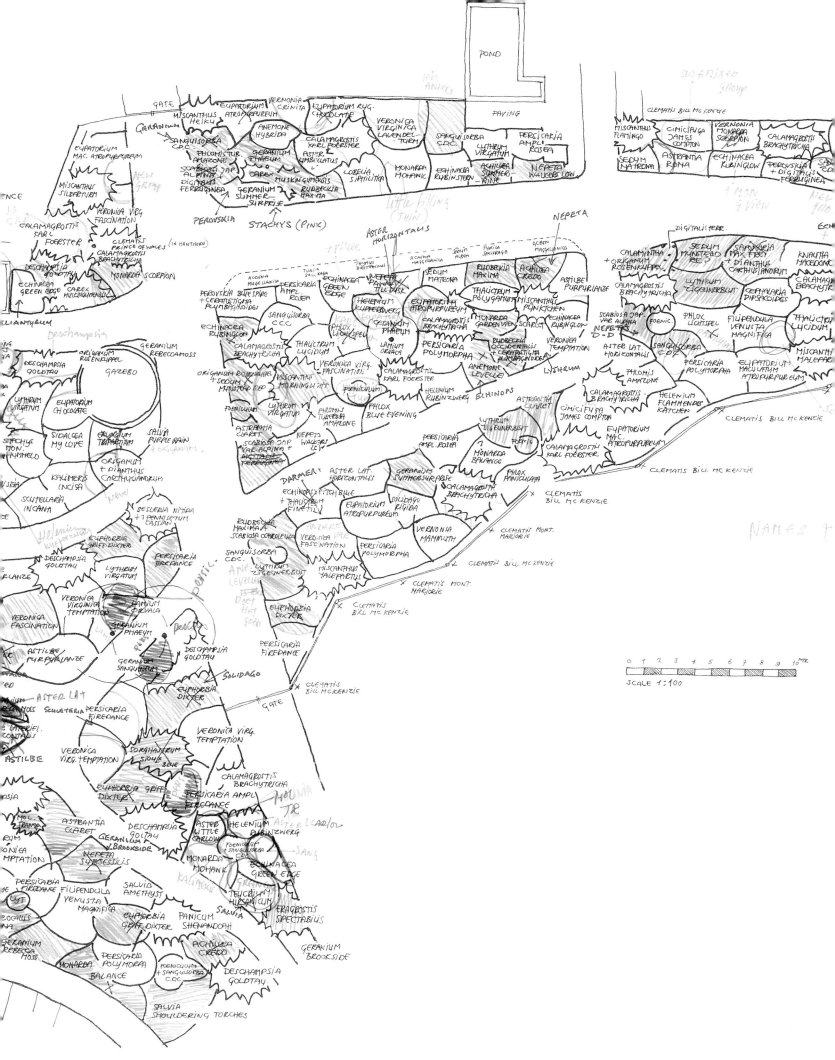

POND

PAVING

GATE
EUPATORIUM ATROPURPUREUM
MISCANTHUS HEIKU
VERNONIA CRINITA
EUPATORIUM RUG. CHOCOLATE
VERONICA VIRGINICA LAVENDEL-TURM
SANGUISORBA CDC
PERSICARIA AMPL ROSEA

ORANGED GROUP
CLEMATIS BILL MC KENZIE
MISCANTHUS FLAMINGO
CIMICIFUGA JAMES COMPTON
VERNONIA MONARCA SCORPION
CALAMAGROSTIS BRACHYTRICHA

GERANIUM
SANGUISORBA CDC
PHLOMIS TUB.
ANEMONE HYBRIDA
GERANIUM PHAEUM
CALAMAGROSTIS KARL FOERSTER
ASTER UMBELLATUS
LOBELIA SIPHILITICA
MONARDA MOHANIC
ECHINACEA RUBINSTERN
ACHILLEA SUMMER-WINE
LYTHRUM VIRGATUM
NEPETA WALKERS LOW

EUPATORIUM MAC. ATROPURPUREUM

SEDUM NATRONA
ASTRANTIA RONA
ECHINACEA RUBINGLOW
PEROVSKIA + DIGITALIS FERRUGINEA
SAN

MISCANTHUS SILBERTURM
NEW GROUP
SCABIOSA JAP. ALPINA + DIGITALIS FERRUGINEA
CAREX MUSKINGUMENSIS
GERANIUM SUMMER SURPRISE
RUDBECKIA MAXIMA

+ MON 9 VIEW
NEW GROUP

VERONICA VIRG FASCINATION
PEROVSKIA
STACHYS (PINK)

LITTLE FILLING (THIN)

NEPETA

DIGITALISTEAR
ECH

CALAMAGROSTIS KARL FOERSTER
CLEMATIS PRINCE OF WALES (IN HAWTHORN)
CALAMAGROSTIS BRACHYTRICHA
ASTER HORIZONTALIS
+ FILLER
ACAENA MAGELLANICA
SEDUM ALPIUM
TUNICA SAXIFRAGA
ACAEN MAGELLANICA
CALAMINTHA + ORIGANUM ROSENKUPPEL
SEDUM MUNSTEAD RE.?
SAPONARIA MAX FREY + DIANTHUS CARTHUSIANORUM
KNAUTIA MACEDONC

DESCHAMPSIA GOLDTAU
MONARDA SCORPION
ACAENA MAGELLANICA
PEROVSKIA BLUESPIRE + CERATOSTIGMA PLUMBAGINOIDES
PERSICARIA AMPL. ROSEA
TUNICA SAXIFRAGA
THYMUS BRITTANICUS
ECHINACEA GREEN EDGE
NEPETA PAWNA TILL DUSK
SEDUM MATRONA
RUDBECKIA MAXIMA
ACHILLEA CREDO
ASTILBE PURPURLANZE
LYTHRUM ZIGEUNERBLUT
DIANTHUS CARTHUSIANORUM
CALAMAGROSTIS BRACHYTRICHA
CEPHALARIA DIPSACOIDES
THALICTRUM LUCIDUM

ECHINACEA GREEN EDGE
CAREX MUSKINGUMENSIS
HELIANTHEMUM
DESCHAMPSIA
ECHINACEA RUBINGLOW
CALAMAGROSTIS BRACHYTRICHA
SANGUISORBA CCC
HELENIUM KUPFERZWERG
PHLOX LICHTSPEL
GERANIUM PHAEUM
EUPATORIUM ATROPURPUREUM
THALICTRUM POLYGANUM
MISCANTHUS PUNKTCHEN
MONARDA GARDEN VIEW
ECHINACEA RUBINGLOW
SCABIOSA JAP. VAR ALPINA
NEPETA D-D
FOENIC
PHLOX LICHTSPEL
FILIPENDULA VENUSTA MAGNIFICA
MISCANTH MALEPAR

ORIGANUM ROSENKUPPEL
GERANIUM REBECCA MOSS
GAZEBO
THALICTRUM LUCIDUM
LAMIUM ORVALA
PERSICARIA POLYMORPHA
CALAMAGROSTIS KARL FOERSTER
RUDBECKIA OCCIDENTALIS + CERATOSTIGMA PLUMBAGINOIDES
VERONICA TEMPTATION
ASTER LAT. HORIZONTALIS
PHLOMIS AMAZONE
SANGUISORBA CDC
PERSICARIA POLYMORPHA

DESCHAMPSIA GOLDTAU
ORIGANUM ROSENKUPPEL + SEDUM MUNSTEAD RED
MISCANTHUS MORNINGLIGHT
YERONICA VIRG. FASCINATION
ANEMONE LEVELLEI
HELENIUM RUBINZWERG
ECHINOPS
ASTRANTIA CLARET
CIMICIFUGA JAMES COMPTON
CALAMAGROSTIS BRACHYTRICHA
HELENIUM FLAMMENDES KATCHEN
EUPATORIUM MACULATUM ATROPURPUREUM

LYTHRUM VIRGATUM
EUPATORIUM CHOCOLATE
FOENICULUM
LYTHRUM VIRGATUM
PHLOMIS TUBEROSA AMAZONE
PHLOX BLUE EVENING
FOENICULUM
CALAMAGROSTIS KARL FOERSTER
LYTHRUM ZIGEUNERBLUT
FOENIC
CALAMAGROSTIS KARL FOERSTER
EUPATORIUM MAC. ATROPURPUREUM
CLEMATIS BILL MC KENZIE

SIDALCEA MY LOVE
ERYNGIUM TRIPARTITUM
SALVIA PURPLE RAIN
+ ORIGANUM
ASTRANTIA CLARET
NEPETA WALKERS LOW
PERSICARIA AMPL. ROSEA
MONARDA BALANCE
PHLOX PANICULATA
CLEMATIS BILL MC KENZIE

KALIMERIS INCISA
ORIGANUM + DIANTHUS CARTHUSIANORUM
SCABIOSA JAP. VAR ALPINA + DIGITALIS FERRUGINEA
DARMER?
ASTER LAT. HORIZONTALIS
GERANIUM SUMMER SURPRISE
CALAMAGROSTIS BRACHYTRICHA
CLEMATIS BILL MC KENZIE

SCUTELLARIA INCANA
NAMES +

HELENIUM KUPFER
SESLERIA NITIDA + T PENNISETUM CASSIAN
ECHINOPS FITCH BLUE + THALICTRUM FINETII
EUPATORIUM ATROPURPUREUM
SOLIDAGO RIGIDA
VERNONIA MAMMUTH
CLEMATIS MONT. MARJORIE

EUPHORBIA GRIFF. DIXTER
RUDBECKIA MAXIMA A SCABIOSA OCHROLEUCA
VERONICA VIRG. FASCINATION
PERSICARIA POLYMORPHA
CLEMATIS BILL MC KENZIE

DESCHAMPSIA GOLDTAU
PERSICARIA FIREDANCE
PONTIC.
SANGUISORBA CDC
LYTHRUM ZIGEUNERBLUT
MISCANTHUS YALEPARTUS
CLEMATIS MONT. MARJORIE

LYTHRUM VIRGATUM
ANE LEVELLEI
VERONICA VIRGINIA TEMPTATION
LAMIUM ORVALA
EUPHORBIA DIXTER
CLEMATIS BILL MC KENZIE

VERONICA FASCINATION
GERANIUM PHAEUM
DESCHAMPSIA GOLDTAU
PERSICARIA FIREDANCE

ASTILBE PURPURLANZE
GERANIUM SANGUINEUM
EUPHORBIA DIXTER
SOLIDAGO

ASTER LAT
SCUTELLARIA
PERSICARIA FIREDANCE
CLEMATIS BILL MC KENZIE

ASTILBE
VERONICA VIRG. TEMPTATION
GATE

VERONICA VIRG. TEMPTATION
SORGHASTRUM SIOUX BLUE
CALAMAGROSTIS BRACHYTRICHA

EUPHORBIA GRIFF DIXTER
PERSICARIA AMPL FIREDANCE
MOU JR

MOL TRANS
ASTRANTIA CLARET
GERANIUM BROOKSIDE
DESCHAMPSIA GOLDTAU
ASTER LITTLE CARLOW
HELENIUM RUBINZWERG
ASTER 2 CARLOW

RUM
PSIA
NEPETA SUBSESSILIS
FOENICULUM SANGUISORBA CDC
MONARDA MOHAWK
ECHINACEA GREEN EDGE
SANG

VERONICA TEMPTATION
KALIMERIS

PERSICARIA FIREDANCE
FILIPENDULA VENUSTA MAGNIFICA
SALVIA AMETHYST
TEUCRIUM HIRSANICUM
ERAGROSTIS SPECTABILIS

GAULIS
NA
EUPHORBIA GRIFF DIXTER
PANICUM SHENANDOAH
SALVIA
GERANIUM BROOKSIDE

GERANIUM REBECCA MOSS
PERSICARIA POLYMORA
FOENICULUM + SANGUISORBA CDC
ACHILLEA CREDO
DESCHAMPSIA GOLDTAU

MONARDA BALANCE

SALVIA SMOULDERING TORCHES

0 1 2 3 4 5 6 7 8 9 10 MTR
SCALE 1:100

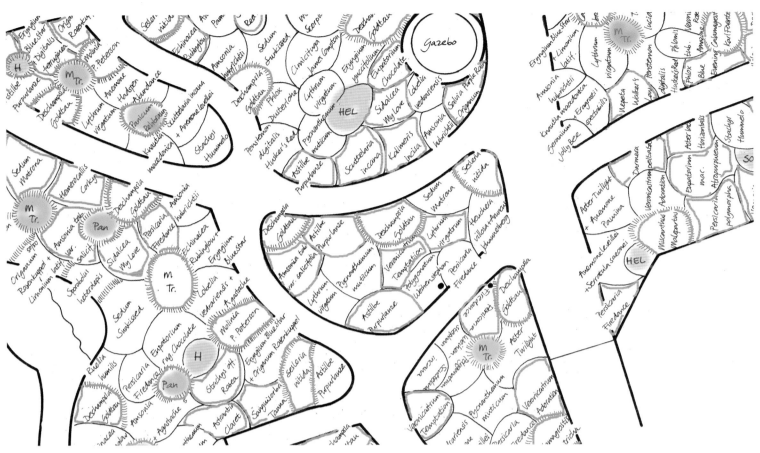

Eupatorium maculatum 'Atropurpureum'

Echinacea purpurea

Eupatorium

Calamagrostis brachytricha

Cimicifuga simplex 'James Compton' after flowering

Cimicifuga simplex 'James Compton' in flower

Astrantia 'Roma'

Sedum 'Matrona'

Sedum

Plant Proportions

# 5,500 m²

Looking out over a bay surrounded by low hills on the southwest coast of Ireland, this garden designed for a private client is expansive and open, a sensation created by a site that is on gently rising ground even while an outer rim of trees provides the sensation of a framework. As some areas of exposed gray bedrock reveal, the soil is not very deep, necessitating careful positioning for the plantings. The garden is not visible from the house, so in the manner of some grand, historic English properties, it is a garden meant to be paid a visit.

The climate is quite different from that of Holland. "Here, there is no winter," says Oudolf. Instead, there is a long growing season, with relatively little difference between summer and winter temperatures. Although this is the driest place in all Ireland, it is still wet by most standards. The site is also buffeted by constant wind so characteristic of the Atlantic coast, sometimes terrifyingly strong but never cold. A soil Oudolf describes as "sandy but also sticky" is, for him, the garden's most familiar element.

The sheer scale of this garden is emphasized by its informality. This is Oudolf's most informal project, in fact, and an example of how far he has come from the roots of Dutch garden design, in which a sense of architecture is ever-present. Although it may seem paradoxical, in his earlier days it would have seemed difficult to conceive of him working within such a loose framework and excluding the architectural elements that have proven to be an integral part of his style.

Planting here exploits the gentle roll of the ground, with clumps of plants forming a hummocky impression. The view from the paths that cut across does, at first, resemble a very characteristic Irish habitat: rough pasture with coarse grasses, mounds of purple heather, and clumps of meadowsweet. The "heather" is, in fact, nothing of the sort but a summer profusion of perennials with flowers in the pink to mauve to purple spectrum, including varieties of *Astilbe*, *Salvia*, *Stachys officinalis*, and *Veronicastrum virginicum*.

The wind has curtailed expression of that favorite Oudolf device: the tall perennial. "There are few plants here taller than 1.2 meters," he says, "but *Stipa gigantea* is particularly effective, plus some *Veronicastrum*, and in spring there are *Eremurus*." *Eremurus* are bulbs whose dramatic flower spikes are up to 2 meters tall, but their season is short; the bulk of this planting needed to be more weather resilient. Forty percent is of grasses, which are truly wind tolerant.

The planting is designed in layers, as with much of his large-scale modern work. The underlying layer is composed of blocks of perennials; the upper layer is a "scatter layer," with firmly structural plants making a disproportionately strong impact for their numbers. Oudolf found the grass *Stipa gigantea* particularly effective, as it rises to around 2 meters, well above the general maximum height. In early summer, when a large number of the flowering perennials are at their most spectacular, its see-through panicles of oatlike flowers rise high over everything else, conjuring a feeling of dreamy romanticism.

County Cork Garden, Ireland, 2006

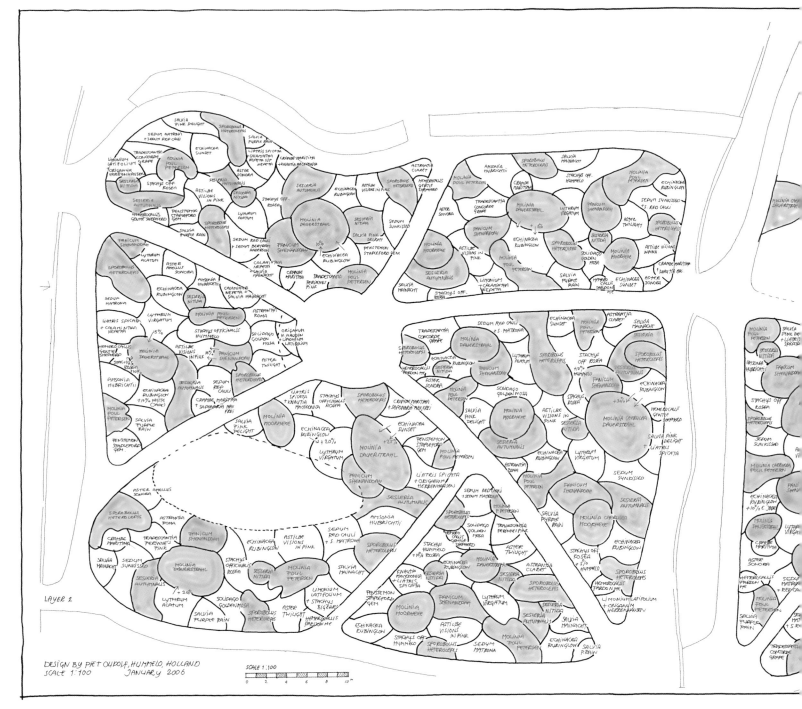

23

LAYER 2

DESIGN BY PIET OUDOLF, HUMMELO, HOLLAND
SCALE 1:100          JANUARY 2006

SCALE 1:100

0   2   4   6   8   10m

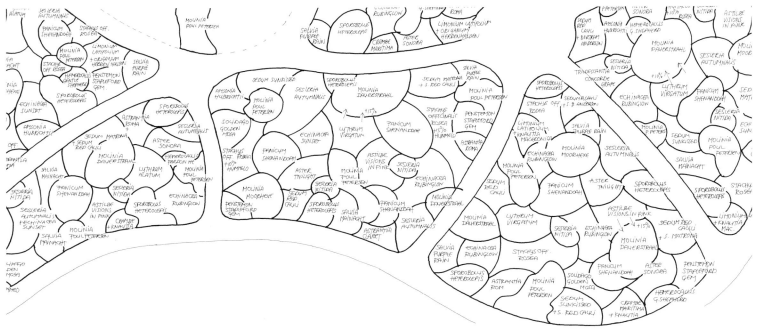

**Trees and shrubs**
**Populus nigra 'Italica,' Salix alba, Crataegus monogyna**

**Lawn**

**Astilbe 'Visions in Pink'**

**Stipa gigantea**

**Helenium 'Rubinzwerg'**

**Aster 'Twilight'**

**Stachys officinalis 'Rosea'**

**Selinum wallichianum**

**Agastache 'Blue Fortune'**

**Knautia macedonica**

**Knautia macedonica leaves**

**Plant Proportions**

# 6,000 m²

This house has a view over the garden to the banks of the Rhine, but the garden in the foreground is so lush with color and texture that visitors often remark it first. The garden is given completely over to perennial planting arranged in a series of roughly rectangular beds covering around 2,500 square meters. Traditional lawn is limited to wide paths between the beds, and an area between the house and the distant view of the river. On the other side of the house, there is a smaller area where more borders have been added to an existing pattern around the drive, including an elongated island bed.

Given the main garden's rectangular site, the decision was made to create a series of plantings that would take the form of geometric island beds, but in a trapezoidal, rather than a more expected, shape. Though meadow-inspired planting combinations dominate, there are also several areas that are shaded by the house or trees. Here woodland perennials were planted, such as varieties of *Actaea*, *Anemone x hybrida*, and ferns, along with light-shade-tolerant shrubs, including varieties of *Hydrangea* and *Corylopsis*.

Taller perennials and grasses appear in a bed that runs down the eastern boundary, while on the western side, a wide border is themed with medium-height clump-forming grasses, such as *Sporobolus heterolepis* and *Pennisetum orientale* 'Tall Tails,' which are repeated in two other island beds. The greatest impact, though, comes through the use of the grasses *Sesleria autumnalis* and *S. nitida*. Both have attractive light-green leaves, which "light the place up, are good through the whole year, and work well with color," Oudolf says. In a striking island bed surrounded by the driveway, *S. autumnalis* is used as a matrix for clumps of *Salvia* cultivars and other grasses. *Sesleria* foliage combines well with flowering perennials, seeming to intensify the colors of even very subtly colored perennial species found elsewhere in the garden such as *Eryngium yuccifolium* and *Echinacea purpurea* 'Green Edge.'

Riverside Residence, Bonn, Germany, 2006

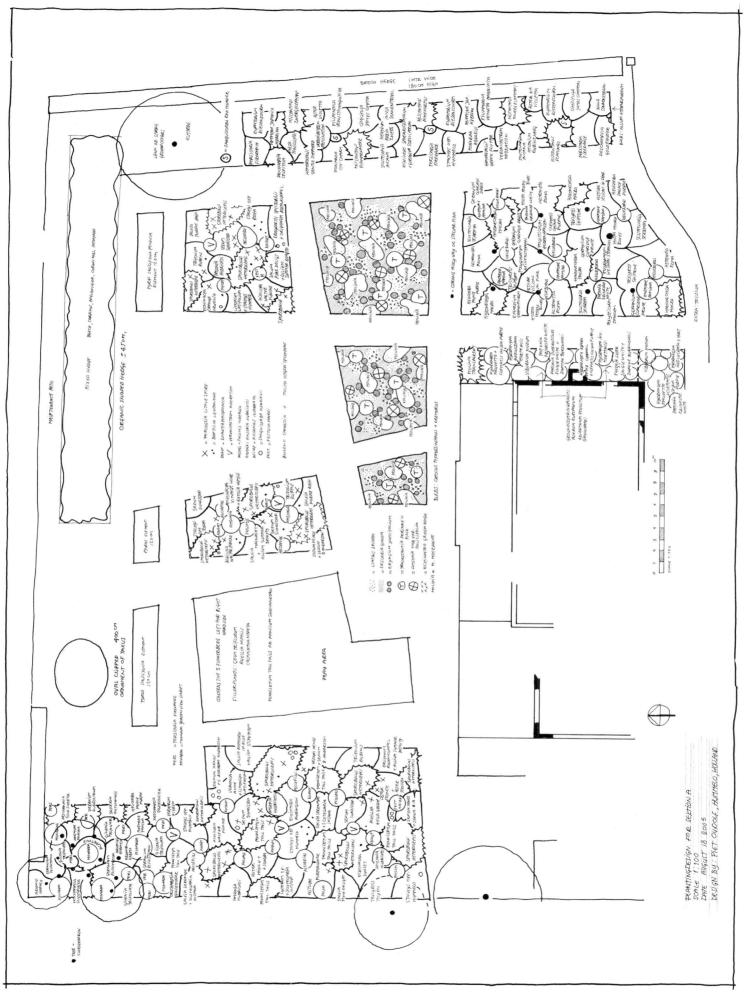

PLANTINGDESIGN FOR SECTION A
SCALE 1:100
DATE AUGUST 18 2005
DESIGN BY: PIET OUDOLF, HUMMELO, HOLLAND

139

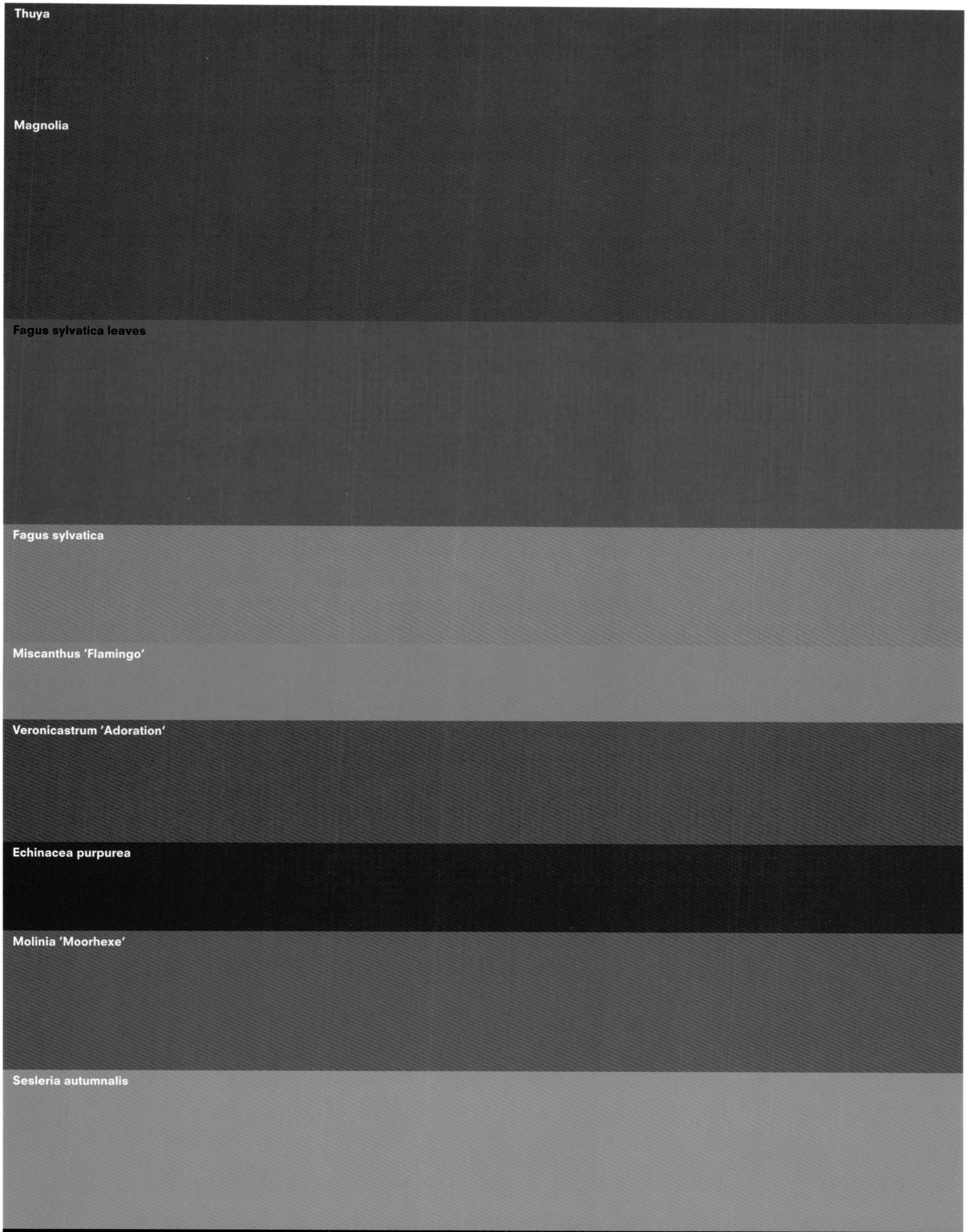

Thuya

Magnolia

Fagus sylvatica leaves

Fagus sylvatica

149

Miscanthus 'Flamingo'

Veronicastrum 'Adoration'

Echinacea purpurea

Molinia 'Moorhexe'

Sesleria autumnalis

**Plant Proportions**

# 8,000 m²

Regeneration of urban spaces is an ongoing project for many city authorities, including Stockholm's. This 8,000-square-meter park is in a working-class, residential area of the city with very high-density apartment blocks and rather bald areas of grass and trees. Oudolf was commissioned by Stefan Mattson, who, as head of parks in Enköping, had also commissioned the Dream Park. The plan is for the creation of high-intensity perennial planting that fits into the existing use of the site, by recognizing the "desire paths" local residents have trodden into the grass. Sweden is famous for the quality of its public housing, and many of its cities have stunning public gardens adjacent to individual blocks of high-density, low-income housing.

"I wanted this simple idea of concentric circles to give a different perspective from wherever you stand," Oudolf says. Most of the site is in the sun, but areas around existing mature trees feature shade-tolerant plants: ferns, species of *Aruncus*, and a ground cover of *Asperula odorata* and *Brunnera macrophylla* 'Jack Frost.' The main area, though, is based on five concentric zones of planting, each approximately 3 meters wide, centered around seating, a water feature, and a pool designed to be shallow enough for children to wade in.

The planting zones here are broadly similar in principle to those that Oudolf has been experimenting with since his work at Wisley in 2001. "The plants in each circle should work well with each other, as well as with neighboring ones," he says. Sometimes the plant combination is relatively straightforward. For example, the use of *Calamintha nepeta* subsp. *nepeta* with *Molinia caerulea* 'Moorhexe' pairs a very effective ground-cover plant with a grass, which will eventually be the dominant element. Other combinations are more complex: one includes a 60:40 mix of *Lythrum virgatum* and *Briza media*—an upright pink perennial with a grass—interspersed with *Astilbe* 'Visions in Pink' and *Geranium* 'Sirak,' both of which are also pink but bloom earlier than the lythrum. These plants are also dotted into blocks of the grass *Molinia caerulea* 'Heidebraut,' which alternate with the lythrum/briza combination.

Dot plants occupy only a small area but make a disproportionately strong impact for their size. In many cases, these are structural over a long season, such as the grass *Festuca mairei*. In other cases, they are for creating splashes of color at an earlier season than the bulk of the surrounding planting, as with the bold early-summer pink of *Geranium* 'Sirak.'

Skärholmen Park, Stockholm, Sweden, 2010

water feature : rock pool
natural stone

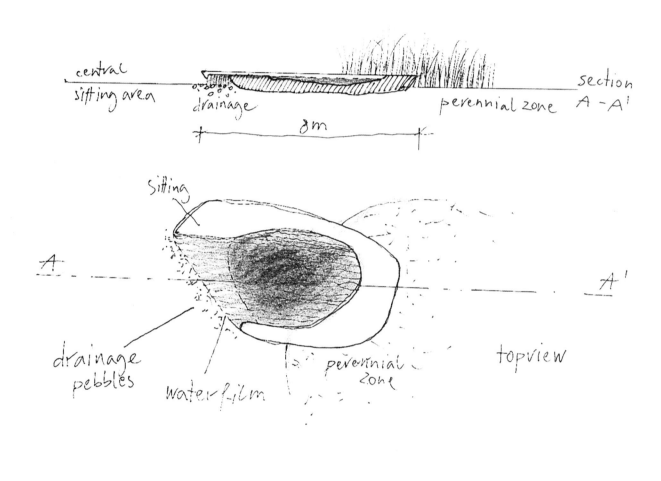

central
sitting area

drainage

8m

perennial zone

section
A - A¹

Sitting

A

A¹

drainage
pebbles

water film

perennial
zone

topview

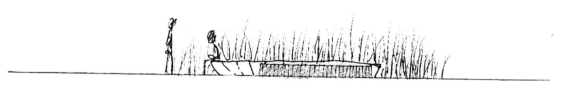

6m

frontview

1:200

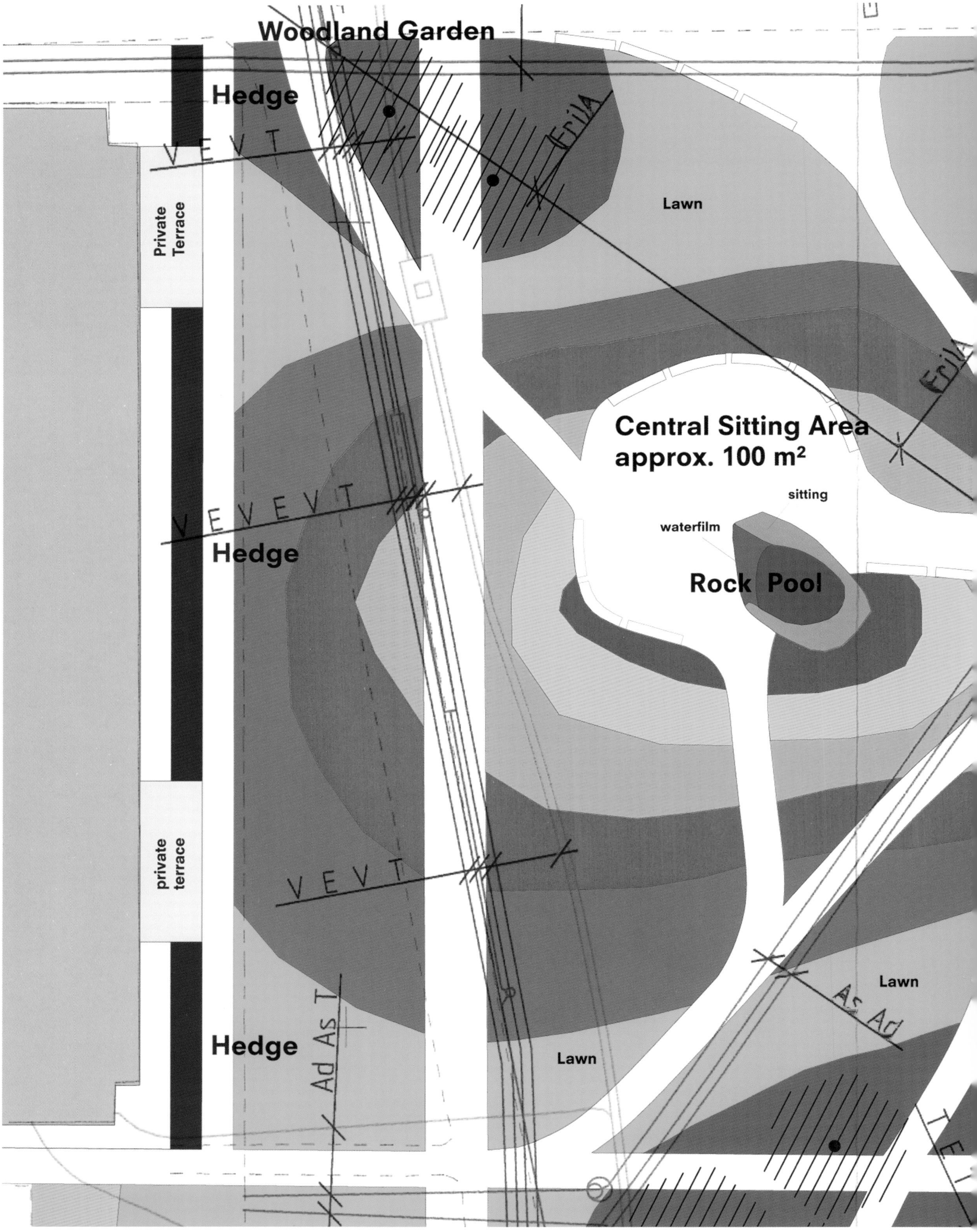

**Woodland Garden**

**Hedge**

Private Terrace

V E V E V T

**Hedge**

Erila

Lawn

**Central Sitting Area
approx. 100 m²**

sitting

waterfilm

**Rock Pool**

ErilA

152

V E V E V T

private terrace

V E V T

Ad As T

**Hedge**

Lawn

As Ad

Lawn

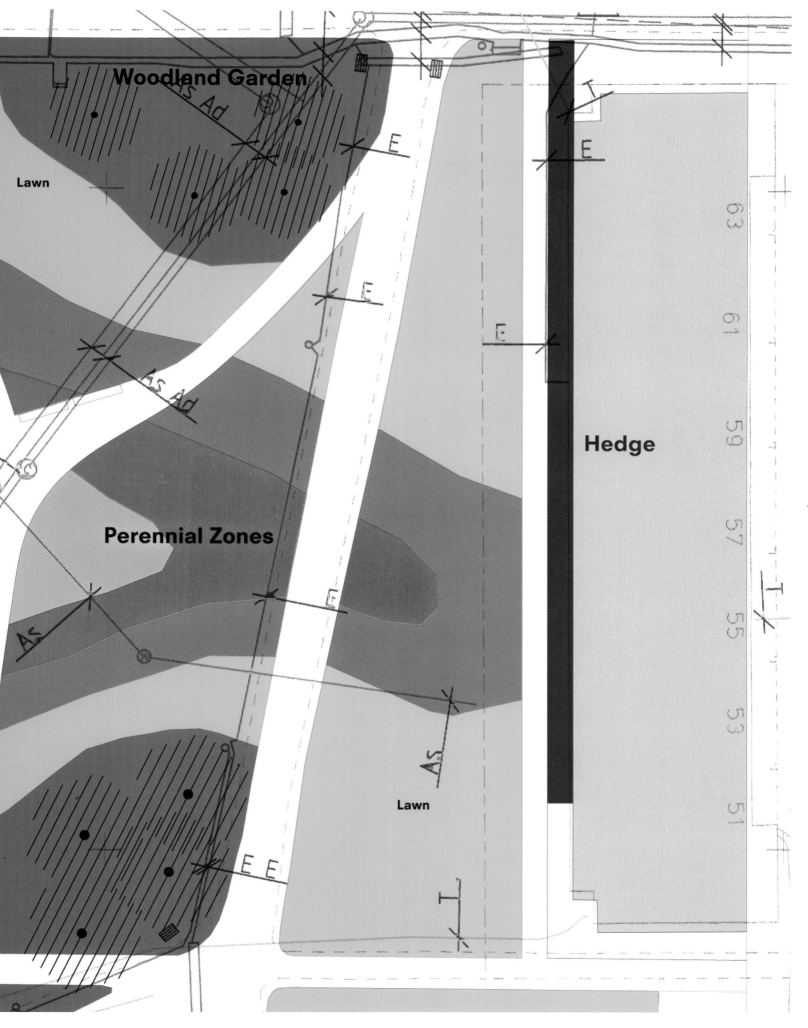

**Woodland Garden**

Lawn

**Perennial Zones**

**Hedge**

Lawn

fill up with
Heuchera villosa 30%
Sesleria autumnalis 70%

30 Heuchera
50 Sesleria

GN
GN 40
GN 15
GN 16
GN 12

lawn

lawn

A3

epi 45
epi
epi
epi
epi

Des
Des
Des

A2

g+3
epi
Des 13
SO1

epi

110 Asperula
35 Brunnera

405 Asperula
140 Brunnera

154

lawn

**SKÄRHOLMENS PERENNPARK**
Stockholm Sweden

E2
Ech 45/5
St 33 ses 10
Sed 37 cal 21
Ech 62/7
S
H 26
B 8
G
H 14
H
L 5
B 20
H 49
G
PA
Sed 22 cal 24
S
St 25 ses 8
Ech 41/5
PA
Sed 31 cal 17
St 30 ses 9
S
PA
Ech 60/7
S
Sed 46 cal 25
Sed 10 cal 5
Sed 37

E1
Sed 25 cal 14
PA
St 48 ses 15
Ech 72/8
PA
S
PA
H
Sed
PA
St 51 ses 16
H 30
PA
Ech 81/9
H
S
G
L 31 B 21
H 48
PA
Sed 41 cal 23
PA
St 33 ses 10
G
L 37 B 24
S
Ech 53/6
H
Sed 49 cal 24
S
St 21 ses 6
PA
Ech 88/10
S
H
Sed 35
PA
St 38 ses 12
Sed 56 cal 31
PA
Ech 70/8
Sta 36 cal 19 ses 11
30/3 Ech
S

E2a
Ech 84
Path
L 3
P3
8 aster 4 echinops
H 40
L 25 B 17
17 L 11 B
G
H
L 4 B 3
L 13 B 8
P
S
L 1 B 8
P
27 Sta + Lim 12
P
81 Sedum Sunkised
S
18 Sta + Lim
17 7 St + Lim
62 Sedum Sunkised
S
17 St Lim
Path
P
P
P
P
P
P
P
141 Mol. Myrrhexe
141 Kal: nepeta
16 St + Lim 7
60 Sedum Sunkised
S
16 St + Lim 7
P2
P
H
437 Aster Harry Smith
235 30% Echinops Veitch blue
H 26
L 68 B 46
G
H 63
L 50 B 34
H
H 64
L 52 B 35
H 16
L1
Ech 46/5
S
PA
Sed 91 cal 50
H
St 601 ses 18
St 27 ses 8
PA
E6
Ech 41/5
Ech 43/5
S

lawn

Pond

Echinops
93 Ast.
50 Echin.
H 57
P
L 41 B 27
P4
E

P
P
P

M2
14 Sedum
9 Sta + Lim 4
P
S
18 Sta + Lim 8
S
Sta + Lim
122 Mol. Mooihexe
29 Cal. nepeta
126 Sedum Sunkised
18 8 Sta + Lim
Sedum Sunk.
M1
S
11 Sta + Lim
S2
Sta + Lim 10 4
S1
P5
P
136 Aster
73 Echinops
P
P
H
H
L 26 B 18
H 10
H 14
G
H 20
L 37 B 24
L5
G
L6
PA
S
PA
Sed 41 cal 23
E7
22 St 7 ses
Ech 69/8
S

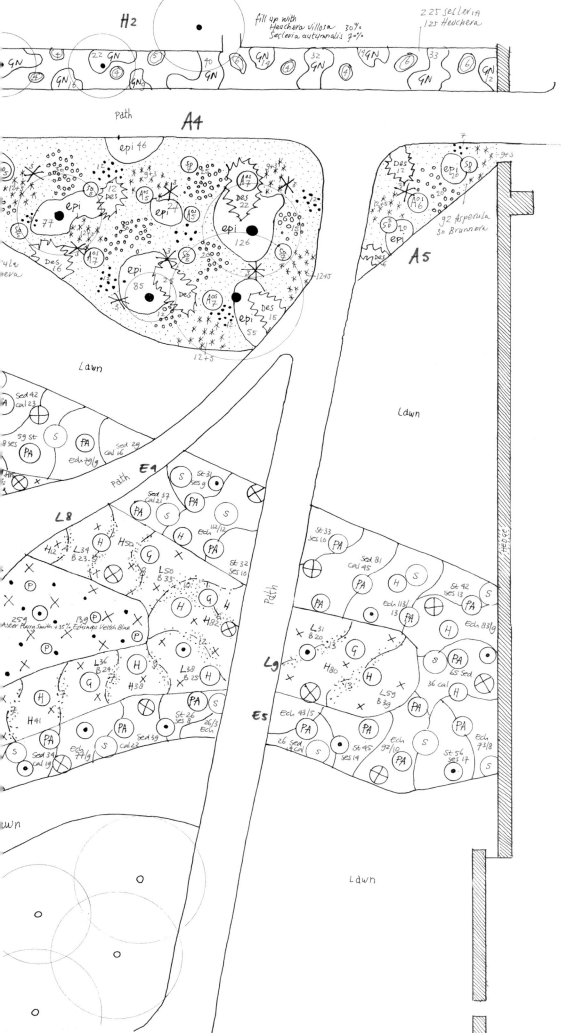

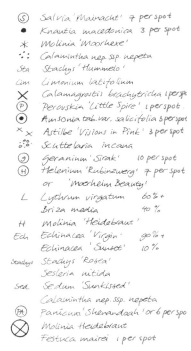
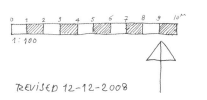

155

REVISED 12-12-2008

Vårbergsvägen

# 10,000 m²

Chicago's Lurie Garden is part of the tradition of intensively maintained garden areas within a larger and more extensive park. Millennium Park is in a key downtown location, and it includes dramatic large-scale contemporary sculptures by Anish Kapoor and Jaume Plensa, as well as a bandstand by architect Frank Gehry.

The 2.5-acre garden was a collaboration between landscape architecture firm Gustafson Guthrie Nichol and set and lighting designer Robert Israel, who worked on the garden's overarching concept. The whole site is treated as a work of art whose central concept depends heavily on Oudolf's planting. A broad boardwalk symbolizing the wooden sidewalks that once lined the city's streets and a narrow waterway referred to as the "Seam" divide the site into two distinct regions of planting: the "Dark Plate" and the "Light Plate." The Dark Plate is an area of open woodland richly underplanted with shade-tolerant plants, symbolizing the wild landscape that existed before the arrival of white settlers. Considerably larger and set at a lower level is the more open area of the Light Plate, featuring gently rolling ground with small clumps of perennials, creating an effect of a stylized prairie landscape. The entire area is effectively a giant roof garden, as it stands over an underground parking garage.

A swirling river of blue and violet salvia cultivars stands out as a bold feature in early summer. Dot planting of grasses adds rhythm and repetition, to bring coherence to the whole. Two native grasses are used in this way: *Sporobolus heterolepis* and *Panicum virgatum* 'Shenandoah.' Providing early-summer splashes of color are the perennials *Papaver orientale* 'Scarlett O'Hara' and *Hemerocallis* 'Chicago Apache.'

A clear break with conventional clump planting can be seen at the southern end of the Light Plate, in the "Meadow." Here the planting is more consciously naturalistic, with a higher concentration of grasses and more intermingling of varieties. The Meadow contains many native species; indeed, regional natives make up about half of the garden as a whole, the result of Oudolf's collaboration with Roy Diblik, whose company Northwind Perennial Farm has been a pioneer in the commercial production of natives. The growing season in Chicago is relatively short, so to lengthen it, in autumn 2005 a Dutch colleague of Oudolf's, Jacqueline van der Kloet, planted some sixty thousand bulbs.

Colleen Lockovitch, who was the park's first head horticulturalist, sees the Lurie Garden as having a definite educational aspect. "We have signboards that tell people what is flowering at the moment," she says. "Many people stand and read them." Park employees must also frequently teach visitors about their approach to gardening without cutting back until the end of the year, because "It is a very new type of gardening for many of them," she says.

Lurie Garden, Millennium Park, Chicago, Illinois, 2004

Scale 1/200 m   Feb 22,01   P.O + K4

PLANTING DESIGN FOR THE MONROE GARDEN
SCALE 1:700

PIET OUDOLF AUGUST 2001
GUSTAFSON PARTNERS / OUDOLF / ISRAEL

E = ECHINACEA WHITE
S = SEDUM 'CARMEN'
CH = CHASMANTIUM LATIFOLIUM
O = PAPAVER BEAUTY OF LIVERMORE
X X = POTENTILLA HOPWOODIANA

SP = SPOROBOLUS HETEROLEPIS

= SCHIZACHYRIUM 'THE BLUES'

0 1 2 3 4 5 6 7 8 9 10 MTR

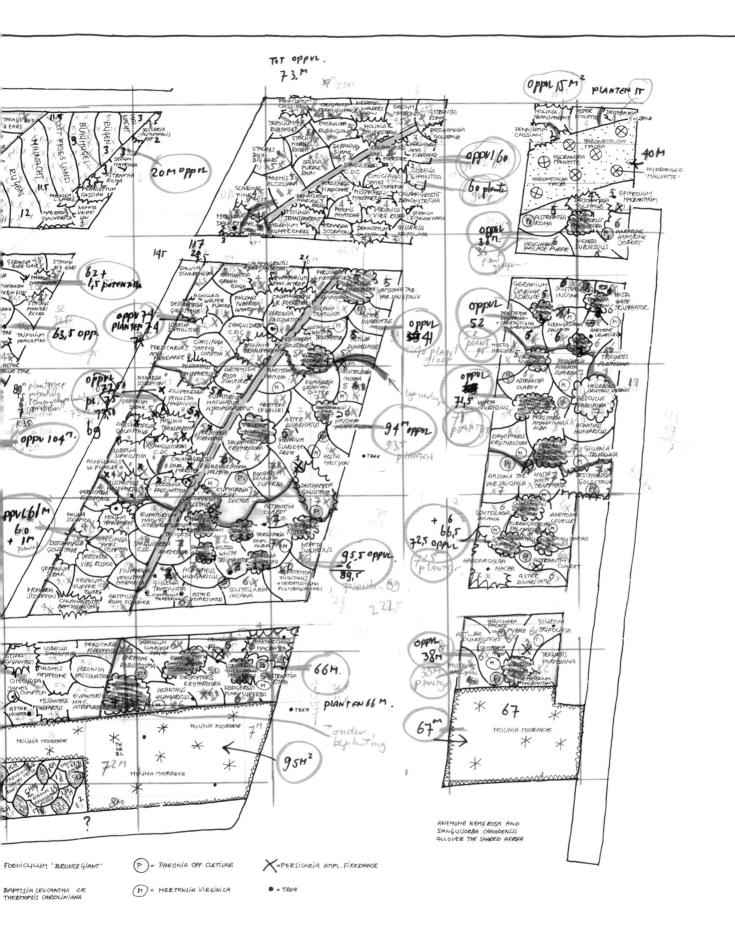

FOENICULUM 'BRONCE GIANT'

⊙ = PAEONIA OFF. CULTIVAR   ✗ =PERSICARIA AMPL. FIREDANCE

BAPTISIA LEUCANTHA OR
THERMOPSIS CAROLINIANA

Ⓜ = MERTENSIA VIRGINICA   ● = TREE

ANEMONE NEMEROSA AND
SANGUISORBA CANADENSIS
ALLOVER THE SHADED AEREA

# 10,000 m²

Designers' gardens are often quite different from the ones they create for clients; for Oudolf the garden at Hummelo is a place for experimentation. "I work in so many different spaces, have so many new ideas," he says. "I try out many things elsewhere and so often want to change the garden at home, as well. It is also very important to be able to show people my ideas." To some extent, the garden is a showroom: potential clients are invited here, and the garden can be seen by the numerous visitors to the nursery that his wife, Anja, runs.

The garden has gone through myriad changes, but its core sense of structure endures. The distinctive yew curtains at the end of the garden, a number of yew hedges, and the beech tunnel have been there since he first developed the garden. Once a central axis plunged down between staggered yew columns through the middle of three off-center oval borders, all surrounded by lawn. In 2003 however, all this was changed, and the whole area filled with perennials. The central axis is still there, now all but invisible beneath planting. Brick paths dictate that visitors walk in circles so the viewpoints from which plants are seen are always changing. The gradual loss of clipped structure and its replacement with perennials reflects the changes in Oudolf's approach to design.

For clients, Oudolf draws detailed plans on large sheets of tracing paper, but here, he says, "I make lists and work out a concept in my mind, and then set plants out by eye." In early- to mid-summer, there is a sense that "many things are happening, but most of it is still to come," he adds. There are only a small number of blooming plants then, for much was designed not to flower until late summer. Everything is nevertheless fresh, with many of the later-developing species forming lush, leafy clumps. Structure is provided by species of verbascum, thalictrum, eryngium, astilbe, and salvia. A lot of color comes from what Oudolf calls "filler" species, which are rather amorphous but fill space and flower plentifully. Geraniums are the most obvious example, along with species of stachys, geum, nepeta, and saponaria.

Late summer and autumn are when the grasses and taller perennials—plants so firmly associated with the Oudolf look—take over, so this is easily considered the garden's high point. The fact that so many of them continue to look good as the weather gets colder has always impressed him, and his promotion of the beauties of dead stems, seedheads, and frost-covered plants has made a considerable impact with gardeners. Now a mecca for plant enthusiasts as well as designers, the Oudolf garden at Hummelo continues to be a design laboratory as well as a decorative garden in its own right.

**Oudolf Garden, Hummelo, The Netherlands, 1982** Onward

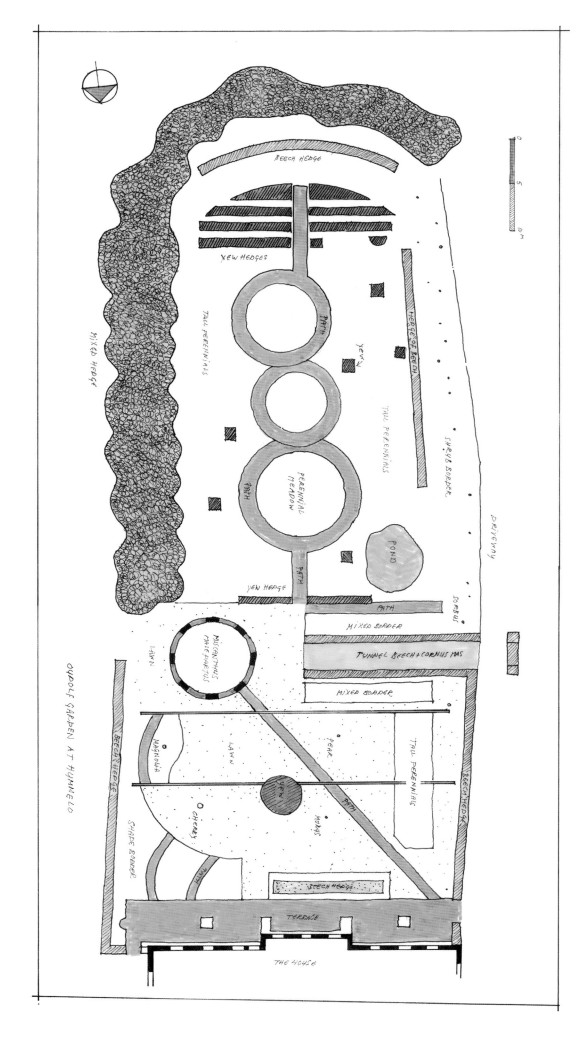

OUDOLF GARDEN AT HUMMELO

BEECH HEDGE

BEECH HEDGE

TERRACE

THE HOUSE

BEECH HEDGE

SHADE BORDER

LAWN

MAGNOLIA

LAWN

CHERRY

YEW

MALUS

PEAR

TALL PERENNIALS

PATH

PATH

MISCANTHUS
MALE PARTS

MIXED BORDER

TUNNEL BEECH + CORNUS MAS

MIXED BORDER

PATH

SORBUS

DRIVEWAY

YEW HEDGE

POND

PERENNIAL
MEADOW

PATH

PATH

PATH

TALL PERENNIALS

SHRUB BORDER

YEW

HEDGE OF BEECH

MIXED HEDGE

TALL PERENNIALS

YEW HEDGES

BEECH HEDGE

0   5   10 M

169

"Looking out over his perennial meadow, Mr. Oudolf articulated it this way: 'You look at this, and it goes deeper than what you see. It reminds you of something in the genes — nature, or the longing for nature.' Allowing the garden to decompose, he added, meets an emotional need in people. 'You accept death. You don't take the plants out, because they still look good. And brown is also a color.'"

— New York Times, January 31, 2008

Taxus baccata leaves

Taxus baccata

Deschampsia 'Goldtau,' Amsonia tabernaemontana var. salicifolia

Plant Proportions

# 11,000 m²

Most of what we see in the landscape is not instantly recognizable as one of a kind. Every now and again though, about once a decade, something comes along that is completely new. The living walls in Japan or Paris are one example of such a paradigm shift, as is the climbing-plant-draped megapergola of Zürich's MFO Park. The High Line in New York City is another. A rusty elevated railway originally built to carry meat and other freight to and from the factories and warehouses of Manhattan's West Side, it was nearly pulled down but was saved by a citizen action group, Friends of the High Line, that saw its potential as a public space.

Landscape architecture firm Field Operations and architecture firm Diller Scofidio & Renfro were given the task of creating the world's first high-level linear park, and Field Operations in turn commissioned Oudolf for the planting design. The High Line had stood two stories high for many years—mostly unknown and unloved apart from graffiti writers and aficionados of wildlife in the city—growing a unique flora, a combination of native species and garden escapees. The irony of the $152 million reconstruction of the first two sections was that everything on the surface had to be taken apart and rebuilt, which involved the removal of all flora. Oudolf's role was to design a plant mix that looked as much like the old spontaneous flora as possible but was also colorful and ornamental. He achieved this by choosing a mix with about one-half native species and with heavy concentrations of grasses and shrubs, to avoid being too ornamental.

The High Line runs between buildings, once noisily industrial, now increasingly upscale residential; sometimes it even seems to disappear as it runs underneath them. It is bathed in light and shade, the latter likely to increase in time as developers inevitably build more and more. Most areas are planted with a mix evoking the perennial-rich grassland that develops on abandoned fields; others with a shrub and perennial mix that evokes the next stage of the succession process, as nature's inexorable drive replaces grasses with woody plants. The design of the planted areas emphasizes the feel of spontaneity—feathered paving makes it look as if the plants are actually beginning to cover the concrete. The design follows a planting pattern where open meadow dissolves into half-open woodland, then into a fuller woodland area of dense, small trees with underplanting to envelop the visitor more fully as the length of the park is traversed.

Summer, especially late summer, sees plenty of color, with the yellow daisies characteristic of so many of the United States's East Coast woodland edge or roadside habitats—e.g., species of *Helenium* and *Helianthus*—alongside the now familiar pink daisies of *Echinacea purpurea*, which has become something of a poster specimen for the native plant movement. As the season progresses, the grasses become more prominent so that they appear to become a matrix, the role that nature grants them in most open habitats; many are native species, such as *Sporobolus heterolepis*, *Bouteloua curtipendula*, and *Panicum virgatum*. Autumn inevitably provides a final splash of color with orange *Amelanchier canadensis*. Winter is surprisingly decorative, with prominent seedheads of plants such as *Liatris spicata* and *Pycnanthemum muticum* set against the paler, wispier grasses.

The High Line, New York, New York, 2009–2010 Phase one

W20TH ST

TENTH AVE

W19TH ST

**5**

Chelsea
Grasslands

W18TH ST

**4**

10th Avenue Square

W17TH ST

Northern Spur Preserve

W16TH ST

Chelsea Market
Passage

Southern Spur

W15TH ST

**3**

Diller – Von Furstenberg
Sundeck

W14TH ST

14th Street
Passage

TENTH AVE

W13TH ST

**2**

Washington
Grasslands

WASHINGTON ST

LITTLE W12TH ST

**1**

Gansevoort
Woodland

GANSEVOORT ST

N

# 11,500 m²

Sitting at the base of the skyscraper massif that is the southern tip of Manhattan, Battery Park looks out over one of America's most iconic sights, the Statue of Liberty. The Battery is New York's oldest waterfront park, its name commemorating a fortification built by the first European settlers, Dutch traders who had named their home "New Amsterdam." Despite its premier location, by the mid-1990s it had become run-down, leading to the establishment of the Battery Conservancy to coordinate its revitalization as well as raise funds for maintenance and operations. The attack on the nearby World Trade Center on September 11, 2001 led the promenade, which had been under construction at the time, to be dedicated as the Gardens of Remembrance to survivors as well as victims.

Given the park's history, it seems fitting that a Dutchman should have been asked to contribute to the existing framework of trees, lawns, and paths. The result was a rare opportunity to create new plantings within a master plan first created in the 1980s by Philip Winslow, leading to a contemporary interpretation of the traditional park. Much of the site is shaded, so there is an emphasis on woodland species and relatively few of the grasses more widely associated with Oudolf's work. One that thrives in the teeth of the wind that can blow in from the sea is *Calamagrostis brachytricha*, whose movement in every breeze is highly expressive. This is a plant originally from Korea, but American native grasses are used too. One, *Panicum virgatum*, might well have grown on this site in presettlement days.

A substantial minority of the plants here are natives, including some sun lovers for the more open areas, such as *Asclepias incarnata* (swamp milkweed) and *Baptisia leucantha* (wild white indigo), a particular favorite of Oudolf's. Native shade tolerators under the trees include *Eurybia divaricata* (white wood aster), a plant familiar to many in the northeast as a key late-summer wildflower, and *Ageratina altissima* 'Chocolate' (white snakeroot), a selection made from another familiar late-summer flowering woodland-edge species. Due to comprehensive nursery propagation of the park's plantings, the gardens at the Battery are not only self-sustaining, but also produce a surplus of new plants that are distributed to other New York City parks.

Wider areas of strongly textural plantings in the internal areas of the park provided the opportunity for more expression. The narrow borders and raised beds along the promenade, a legacy of the previous layout, were more of a challenge to plant, requiring compact species that perform well over a long season, such as varieties of amsonia, sedum, and salvia, which continue to look tidy and structural after flowering.

The Battery, New York, New York, 2005

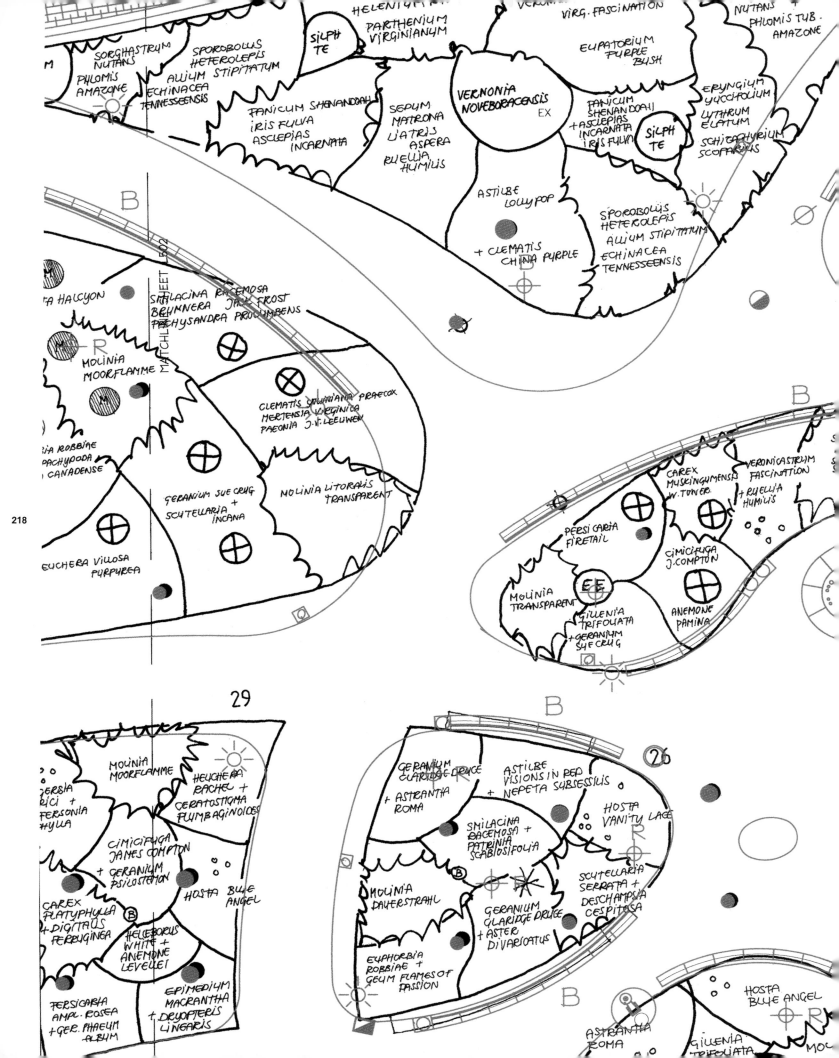

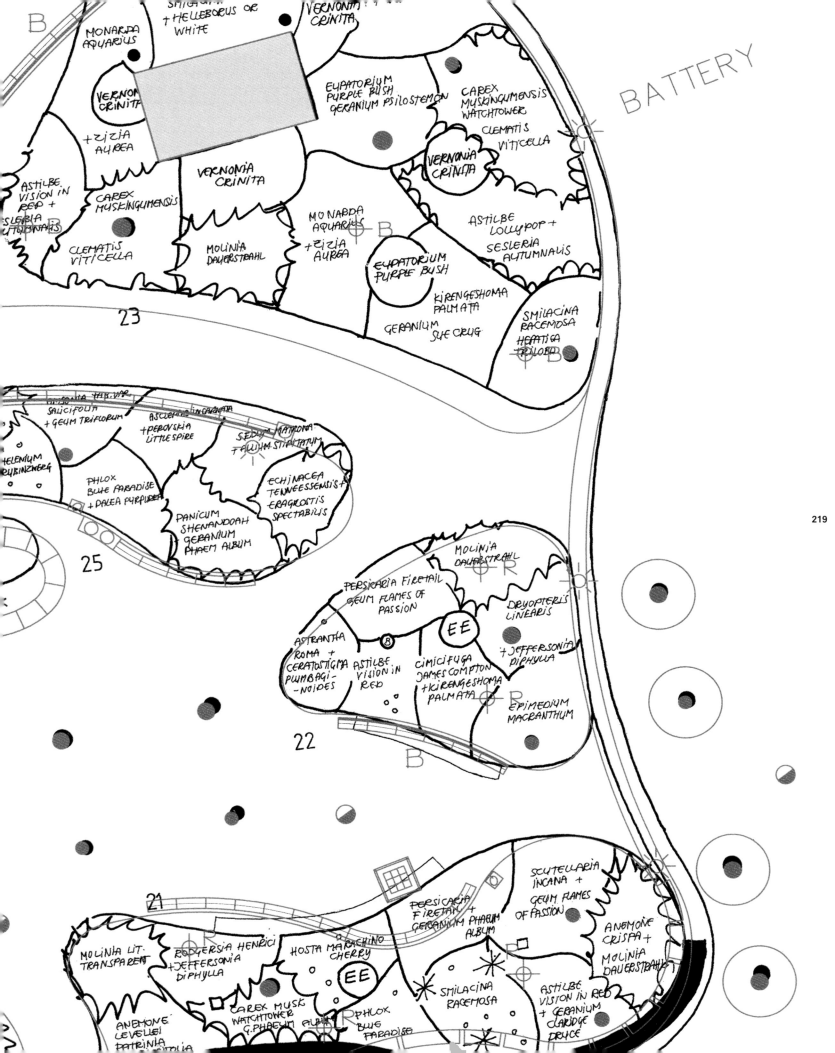

SMILACINA
+ HELLEBORUS OR
WHITE

VERNONIA
CRINITA

MONARDA
AQUARIUS

VERNONIA
CRINITA

EUPATORIUM
PURPLE BUSH
GERANIUM PSILOSTEMON

CAREX
MUSKINGUMENSIS
WATCHTOWER

CLEMATIS
VITICELLA

+ ZIZIA
AUREA

VERNONIA
CRINITA

ASTILBE.
VISION IN
RED +
SESLERIA
AUTUMNALIS

CAREX
MUSKINGUMENSIS

VERNONIA
CRINITA

MONARDA
AQUARIUS

ASTILBE
LOLLYPOP +
SESLERIA
AUTUMNALIS

+ ZIZIA
AUREA

CLEMATIS
VITICELLA

MOLINIA
DAUERSTRAHL

EUPATORIUM
PURPLE BUSH

KIRENGESHOMA
PALMATA

SMILACINA
RACEMOSA
HEPATICA
TRILOBA

GERANIUM
SUE CRUG

23

AMSONIA TAB. VAR.
SALICIFOLIA
+ GEUM TRIFLORUM

ASCLEPIAS INCARNATA
+ PEROVSKIA
LITTLE SPIRE

SEDUM MATRONA
TALICTRUM STRIATUM

HELENIUM
RUBINZWERG

PHLOX
BLUE PARADISE
+ PALEA PURPUREA

ECHINACEA
TENNESSENSIS +
ERAGROSTIS
SPECTABILIS

PANICUM
SHENANDOAH
GERANIUM
PHAEM ALBUM

25

MOLINIA
DAUERSTRAHL

PERSICARIA FIRETAIL
GEUM FLAMES OF
PASSION

DRYOPTERIS
LINEARIS

EE

+ JEFFERSONIA
DIPHYLLA

ASTRANTIA
ROMA +
CERATOSTIGMA
PLUMBAGI-
-NOIDES

ASTILBE
VISION IN
RED

CIMICIFUGA
JAMES COMPTON
+ KIRENGESHOMA
PALMATA

EPIMEDIUM
MACRANTHUM

22

B

SCUTELLARIA
INCANA +
GEUM FLAMES
OF PASSION

21

MOLINIA LIT.
TRANSPARENT

RODGERSIA HENRICI
+ JEFFERSONIA
DIPHYLLA

HOSTA MARACHINO
CHERRY

PERSICARIA
FIRETAIL +
GERANIUM PHAEUM
ALBUM

ANEMONE
CRISPA +

MOLINIA
DAUERSTRAHL

EE

CAREX MUSK
WATCHTOWER
G. PHAEUM ALBUM

PHLOX
BLUE
PARADISE

SMILACINA
RACEMOSA

ASTILBE
VISION IN RED
+ GERANIUM
CLARIDGE
DRUCE

ANEMONE
LEVELLEI
PATRINIA

# 12,300 m²

Once one of Britain's grandest gardens, the Trentham Estate has been reborn as an upmarket visitor destination, with its developers investing in a whole range of new gardens alongside restaurants, shops, and adventure play areas. Leading British garden designer Tom Stuart-Smith was involved from the start, with Land Use Consultants as the master planners; he brought Oudolf on board to add some contemporary planting style.

Central to Trentham is a 1.6-kilometer-long lake, originally part of a naturalistic landscape created in the eighteenth century by the key designer of the time, Lancelot "Capability" Brown. The Victorian era, however, saw the construction of something Brown would have not agreed with: a very formal Italian garden. Stuart-Smith has given this a modern spin with a range of perennials similar in many ways to that used by Oudolf, thereby heavily disguising the ornate layout. Oudolf's work has involved creating some daring yet highly functional new areas, as well as borders on either side of the Italian garden—Stuart-Smith refers to himself as being in a "Piet sandwich" and makes the point that his planting is "intentionally disordered in contrast to the Victorian character of the garden" and that it makes "a good contrast with the more flowing style that Piet has developed." Most intriguing has been what Oudolf calls the "flood plain," an area in the southern part of the garden that is prone to flooding. Plants needed to be tolerant of occasional waterlogging, and the design had to be simple, to allow for rapid recovery or restoration. This difficult design brief inspired a planting pared down to the point of minimalism, an expression of twenty-first-century formality. The area has been coined "Rivers of Grass," a kind of stylized vision of a marshland, with two cultivars of *Molinia caerulea*, 'Edith Dudzus' and 'Heidebraut,' forming great sweeping swathes of fuzzy green from June until August, when the rich brown of the flowers begins to take over, changing to yellow until the seedheads begin to fall in December. For early-summer interest, there is a wide variety of damp-loving plants, including the native bog myrtle, *Myrica gale*, and *Persicaria bistorta*, along with varieties of *Iris*, *Astilbe*, *Trollius*, and *Astrantia*.

In the eastern area, visitors find more of the kind of flower-dominated plantings they have come to expect from Oudolf, namely in the 5,500-square-meter Floral Labyrinth. This is reached through a row of *Betula nigra*, an American birch naturally found on wet soils. Narrow paths weave in and around some thirty individual beds arranged around two areas of lawn, creating the effect of feeling almost overwhelmed by plants. This is deliberate. "It is good to feel the power of nature," Oudolf explains. The effect is amplified by the height of some of the varieties used, e.g., *Thalictrum* 'Elin' for early summer and *Eupatorium maculatum* 'Riesenschirm' for late summer into winter. The lawns are a breathing space rather than the dominant feature or foreground as in traditional garden style, although visitors can use them for picnicking. A variety of perennials are employed as dot plants scattered over the whole area, carefully arranged to provide extra seasonal interest.

Trentham Estate, Staffordshire, England, 2004–2007

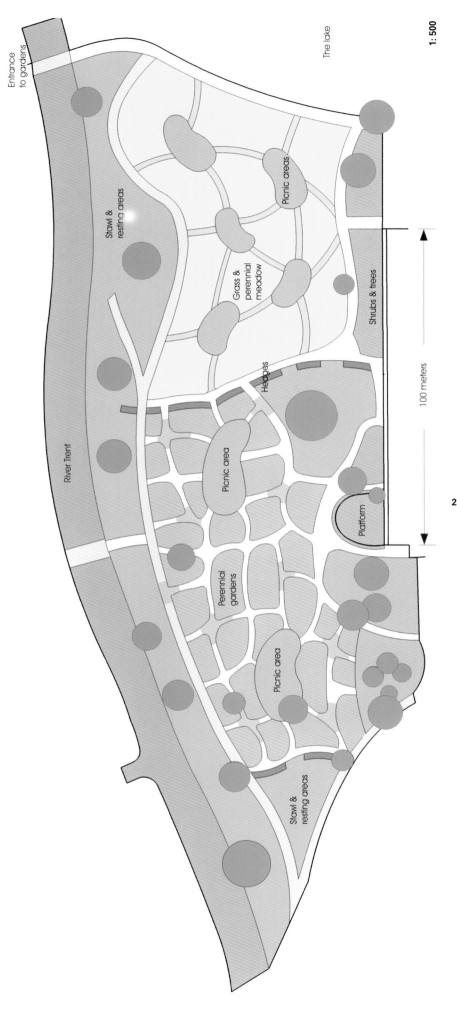

Entrance to gardens

Stawl & resting areas

Grass & perennial meadow

Picnic areas

River Trent

Hedges

Picnic area

Perennial gardens

Picnic area

Platform

Stawl & resting areas

Shrubs & trees

The lake

100 meters

1 : 500

233

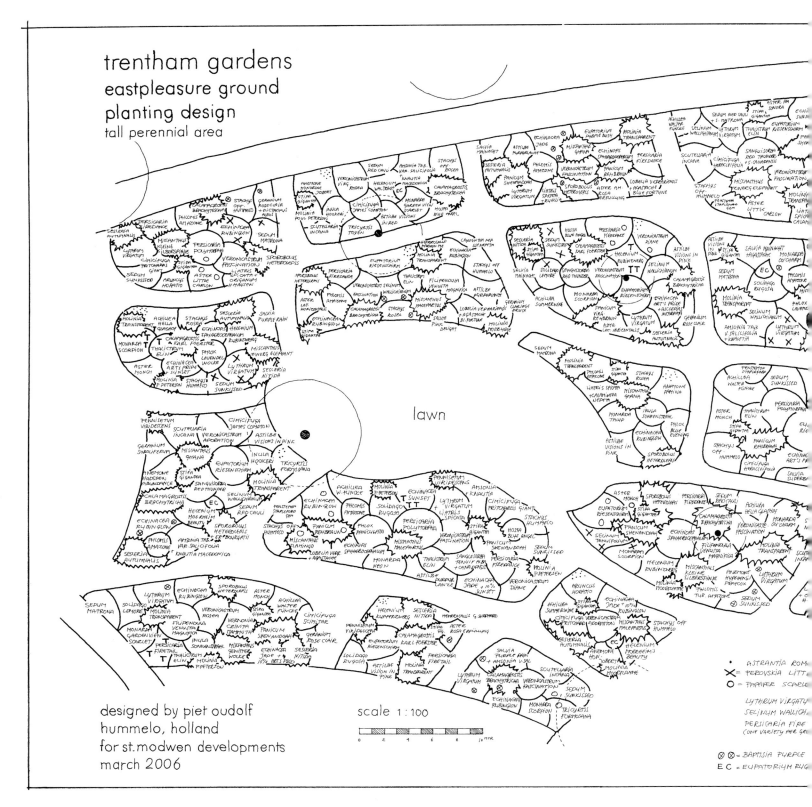

# trentham gardens
## eastpleasure ground
## planting design
### tall perennial area

lawn

designed by piet oudolf
hummelo, holland
for st. modwen developments
march 2006

scale 1 : 100

234

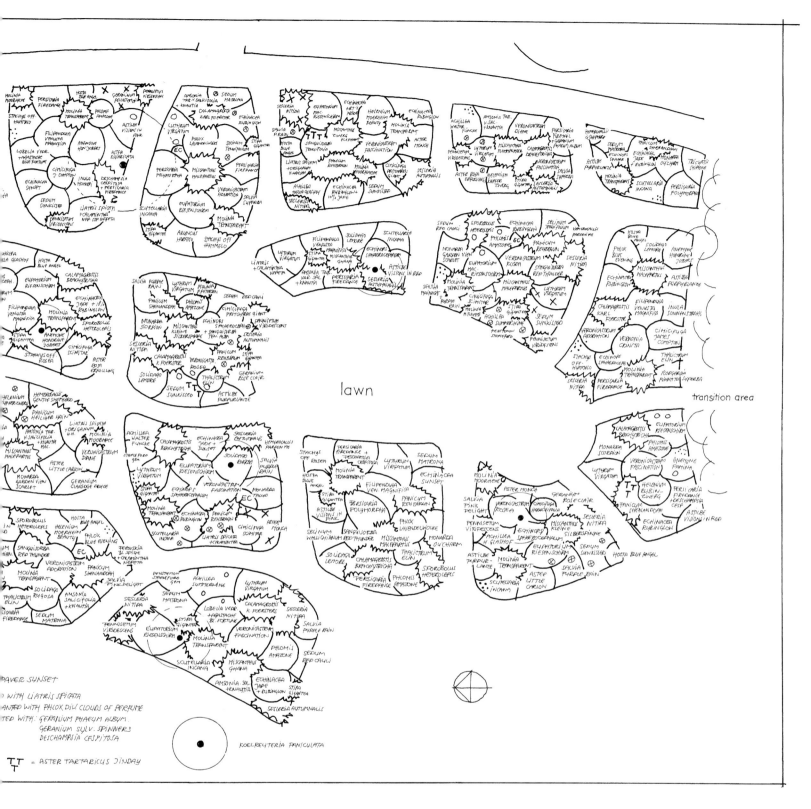

lawn

transition area

235

DAVER SUNSET

D WITH LIATRIS SPICATA

ANTED WITH PHLOX DIV CLOUDS OF PERFUME

TED WITH: GERANIUM PHAEUM ALBUM
GERANIUM SYLV. SPINNERS
DESCHAMPSIA CESPITOSA

T̲T̲T̲ = ASTER TARTARICUS JINDAY

KOELREUTERIA PANICULATA

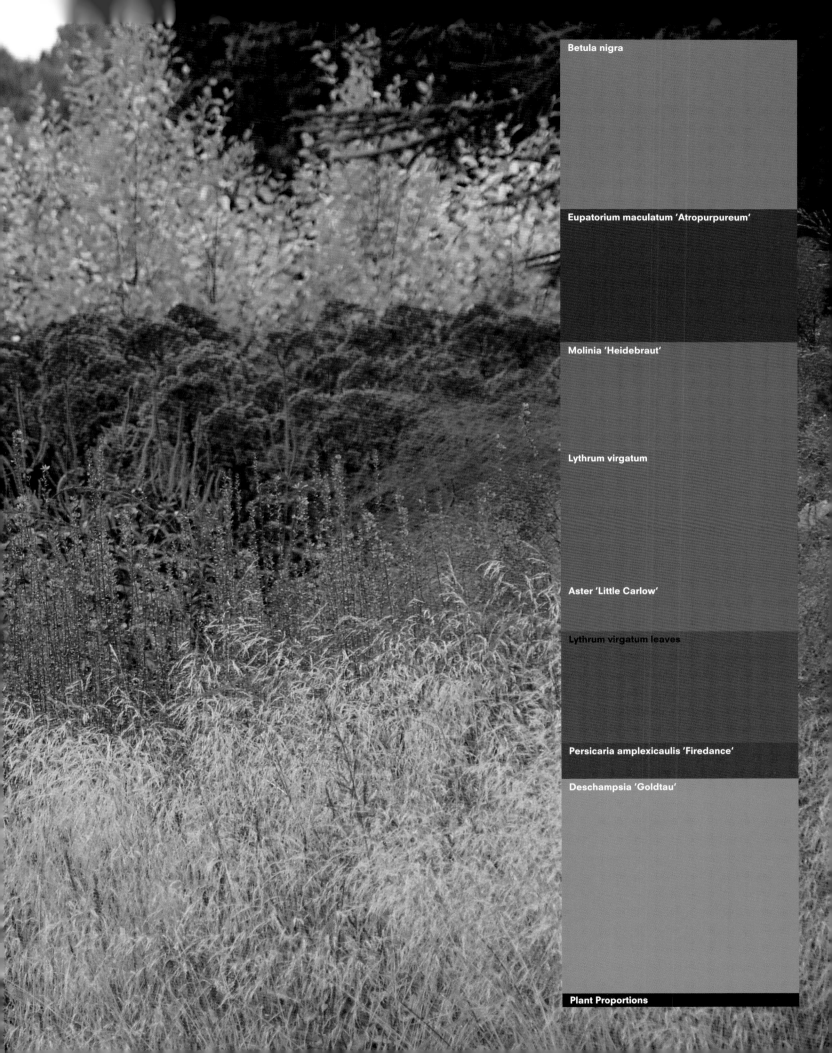

**Betula nigra**

**Eupatorium maculatum 'Atropurpureum'**

**Molinia 'Heidebraut'**

**Lythrum virgatum**

**Aster 'Little Carlow'**

**Lythrum virgatum leaves**

**Persicaria amplexicaulis 'Firedance'**

**Deschampsia 'Goldtau'**

**Plant Proportions**

# 15,000 m²

For centuries English landowners have employed designers to sculpt and order their property, "Capability" Brown (1716–1783) and Humphry Repton (1752–1818) being the two best known. This commission to create a completely new design within a 1.5-hectare walled garden, formerly a vegetable garden, at Scampston Hall in Yorkshire is very much in this tradition, albeit with a distinctly modern twist: the need to create a visitor attraction. Where once cattle and sheep grazed close to the house, now thousands of visitors amble through eight distinct, individual gardens.

From the air the walled garden at Scampston looks much like a vast formal garden of the seventeenth or early eighteenth century. At ground level, however, much of the geometry disappears behind drifts of perennials and flowing waves of grasses, but it is always there, providing a hidden backbone. "I had the idea of creating different garden rooms but on a big scale," Oudolf says. A variety of visions of modernist formality dominate several of these rooms. "Rivers" of the grass *Molinia caerulea* 'Poul Petersen' cover one area, about a sixth of the whole, an idea developed from the "Salvia river" in Enköping. Regular curving bands of the grass alternate with lawn; the regularity can be appreciated in early summer, but as the grass grows and flowers from August onward, the lawn tends to disappear from sight and the area is seen simply as a vast meadow. More conventional material for formal effects appears elsewhere: beech, yew, and lime are employed to create a range of heavily sculptural gardens. History is referenced again in the southwest corner, where a favorite Tudor garden feature, the "mount," is re-created as a flat-topped pyramid; steps lead up to a viewing point, a good place to appreciate this garden's rich patterning. At its base is a wildflower meadow.

The centerpiece of Scampston is a garden dubbed the Perennial Meadow, arranged as a quincunx—a traditional garden layout in which four beds are placed around a central circular bed or oval pond. It has a number of inserts, places where a path leads to a circular seating area where visitors can in turn sit surrounded by color, scent, and in the later months of summer, butterflies. Small groups of perennial varieties are scattered so that as one looks across, the repetition of particularly outstanding colors makes an immediate impact. With a closer look, repeated structures and textures can be seen too, especially in the autumn, as seedheads and russet colors become more dominant.

Adjacent is the Katsura Grove, where woodland plants grow beneath a grid of the Katsura tree *Cercidiphyllum japonicum*. Many woodlanders appear in another feature here: Plantsman's Walk, a 350-meter-long walkway planted with a traditional tunnel of lime. Between that and the outer wall are unusual and rare shrubs and perennials, the kind of plants that do not necessarily fit well into design-led planting schemes. Many of them are choice spring-flowering species that tend to be appreciated for their own singular appeal. Visitors must walk along a section of them from the entrance before being allowed into the central perennial area—a neat way of emphasizing the crucial role of plants in gardens.

Scampston Hall, North Yorkshire, England, 1999

# 25,000 m²

Nantucket Island, off the coast of Massachusetts, has developed recently into a carefully planned and exclusive private residential area. Oudolf started working on a large private garden here in 2007, but only after having brought in landscape architecture firm Field Operations, which has handled the master plan and infrastructure, including the development of some gentle elevation on what was basically a flat site. Parts of the 14-acre site lie only 300 meters from the ocean, making it a challenging location, particularly in terms of finding plant species that will thrive in the windy conditions, and where salt spray can cause considerable damage.

The plan essentially calls for an outer protective ring of woody planting that encloses areas of lawn, perennial meadow, and perennial plantings. A natural swimming pool—dubbed the "kettle hole" after a typical local landscape feature—makes an obvious center point for the garden. The woody planting is designed to develop into two discrete layers: forest trees, including oaks and black locust (*Robinia pseudoacacia*), spaced so that they will eventually merge to form a canopy; and an understory of smaller trees and shrubs, densely planted to resist the wind and develop as a solid mass. Native species of *Crataegus*, *Ilex*, *Vaccinium*, and *Viburnum* have been particularly successful at coping with the prevailing conditions; indeed, a high proportion of the woody planting here is of native origin.

Given the wind, grasses—which simply bend over and bounce back without damage—have proven an especially important part of the planting combinations here. One planting mix uses varieties of *Molinia caerulea* to create a meadowlike matrix, within which are clumps of another grass, *Sporobolus heterolepis*, and a limited palette of flowering perennials as emergents. The sporobolus is used as a matrix species in other areas, and is a native plant, most typically found in relict prairie in the Midwest. In yet other areas, varieties of *Molinia* are used with a higher concentration of perennials and larger grasses. Elsewhere, clumps of varieties of the taller *Calamagrostis* grasses are used, interspersed with flowering perennials to create taller and more borderlike combinations. In the vicinity of the house, these areas of perennials are quite extensive, with paths crisscrossing to create the sensation of walking across a flowering meadow.

With the particularly high concentration of grasses used here, in many cases, flowering perennials appear to be embedded in grasses. This is a sensible approach for a windy coastal environment, and aesthetically it makes for a highly naturalistic appearance.

Nantucket Garden, Massachusetts, 2007–Present

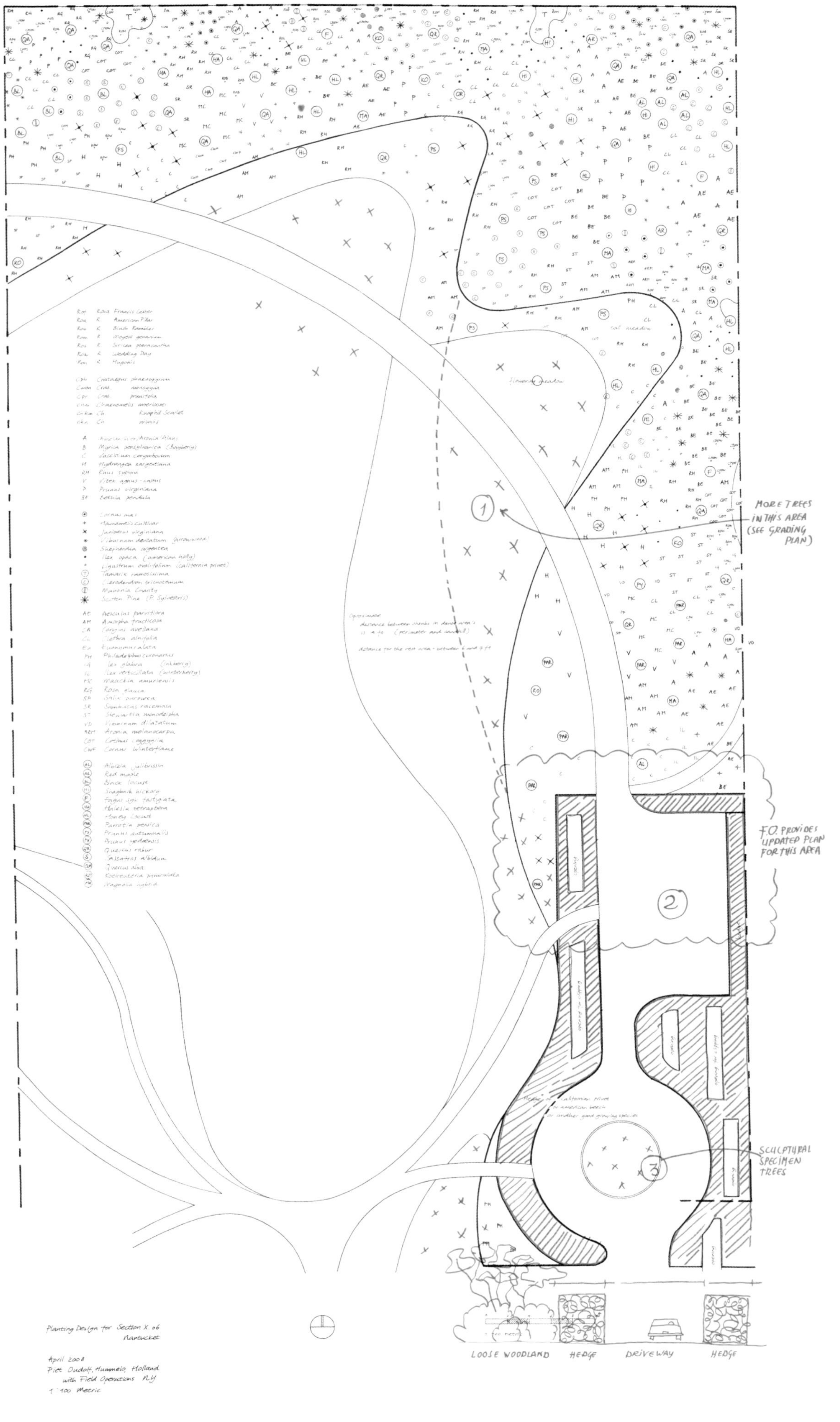

MORE TREES
IN THIS AREA
(SEE GRADING
PLAN)

F.O. PROVIDES
UPDATED PLAN
FOR THIS AREA

SCULPTURAL
SPECIMEN
TREES

(1)

(2)

(3)

LOOSE WOODLAND HEDGE — DRIVEWAY — HEDGE

Planting Design for Section X.06
Nantucket

April 2008
Piet Oudolf, Hummelo, Holland
with Field Operations N.Y.
1:100 Metric

266

**Garage**

Parking

**Gatehouse**

Woodland

Woodland

**Tall Meadow**

Woodland

+26

+25

+28

+28

+26

+28

+28

+28

+27

Woodland

Aquatic Garden

**Pond House**

Perennial Gardens

Tennis Field

Flowering Meadow

Kettle Pond

+31

Lawn

Cobble Beach

Tall Meadow

**Gym**

Croquet Lawn

Putting Green

P C

Woodland

Flowering Meadow

+29

Herb & Vegetable Garden

**Studio**

N

0    25    50        100                    200

Heather's House

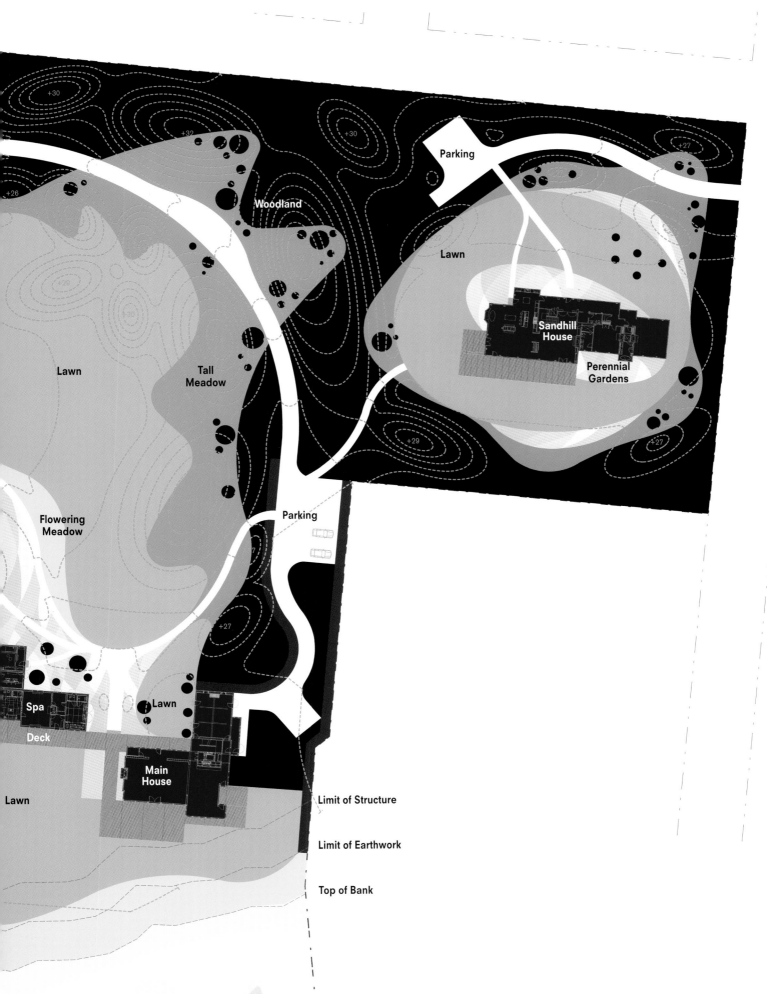

Parking

Woodland

Lawn

Lawn

Tall
Meadow

Sandhill
House

Perennial
Gardens

Flowering
Meadow

Parking

+27

Spa

Lawn

Deck

Main
House

Lawn

Limit of Structure

Limit of Earthwork

Top of Bank

## Trees and Shrubs

| | |
|---|---|
| AC | Acer campestre |
| AG | Acer ginnala |
| AT | Acer truncatum |
| AL | Albizia julibrissin |
| BL | Black Locust |
| CO | Celtis occidentalis |
| CK | Cornus kousa |
| HA | Halesia tetraptera |
| HL | Honey Locust |
| MsHL | Honey Locust multistemmed |
| MA | Magnolia hybrid |
| MAv | Magnolia virginiana |
| NYS | Nyssa sylvatica |
| PAR | Parrotia persica |
| PS | Prunus autumnalis |
| PY | Prunus yedoensis |
| QA | Quercus alba |
| QI | Quercus ilicifolia |
| QP | Quercus palustris |
| QGP | Quercus palustris 'Green Pillar' |
| QR | Quercus robur |
| S | Sassafras albidium |
| ✳ | Scotch Pine |
| STY | Styrax japonica |
| TAX | Taxodium ascendens |
| AE | Aesculus parviflora |
| AM | Amorpha fruticosa |
| ARM | Aronia melanocarpa/arbutif. |
| BE | Betula nigra 'Heritage' |
| BE lk | Betula nigra 'Little King' |
| BE Ms | Betula multistemmed |
| cdi | Callicarpa dichotoma |
| chm | Chaenomeles 'Moerloosei' |
| chn | Chaenomeles nivalis |
| CR | Chionanthus retusus |
| CV | Chionanthus virginicus |
| CLER | Clerodendrum trichotomum |
| CL | Clethra alnifolia |
| ⊙ | Cornus mas |
| c.vir | Cornus sang. 'Viridissima' |
| cwf | Cornus ser. 'Winterflame' |
| COT | Cotinus coggygria |
| CRC | Crataegus crus-galli |
| CRP | Crataegus phaenopyrum |
| CRW | Crataegus 'Winter King' |
| ◓ | Evonymus atropurpureus |
| FM | Fothergilla major |

| | |
|---|---|
| + | Hamamelis vernalis |
| ⊕H | Hydrangea heteromalla |
| ⊕M | Hydrangea mariesii |
| ⊕v | Hydrangea veitchii |
| H | Hydrangea villosa |
| • | Ilex 'Dr. Kassab' / Ilex opaca |
| IG | Ilex glabra (Inkberry) |
| IL | Ilex verticillata (Sparkleberry) |
| ✕ | Juniperus virginiana |
| O | Ligustrum ovalifolium |
| MC | Maackia amurensis |
| b | Myrica pensylvanica (Bayberry) |
| PH | Philadelphus coronarius |
| PT | Populus tremuloides |
| PM | Prunus maritima |
| P | Prunus virginiana |
| RHA | Rhus aromatica |
| RHY A | Rhus typhina size A |
| RHY B | Rhus typhina size B |
| RH | Robinia hispida |
| rc | Rosa carolina |
| rg | Rosa glauca |
| roa | Rosa 'American Pillar' |
| rob | Rosa 'Blush Rambler' |
| rof | Rosa 'Francis Lester' |
| rom | Rosa moyesii geranium |
| ros | Rosa sericea pteracantha |
| row | Rosa 'Wedding Day' |
| rk | Rosa 'Kathleen Harrop' |
| rr | Rosa rugosa white/pink |
| Schy | Schizophragma hydrangeoides |
| ◎ | Shepherdia argentea |
| SP | Salix purpurea |
| SR | Sambucus racemosa |
| STE ps.ca. | Stewartia pseudocamellia |
| ST | Stewartia monadelpha |
| syp | Syringa meyeri palibin |
| syl | Syringa persica laciniata |
| T | Tamarix ramossissima |
| VAC | Vaccinium corymbosum |
| ✳ | Viburnum dentatum (Arrowood) |
| VD | Viburnum dilatatum 'Asian Beauty' |
| VF | Viburnum farreri |
| VN | Viburnum nudum 'Winterthur' |
| VA | Viburnum 'Allegheny' |
| VO | Viburnum trilobum |
| V | Vitex agnus-castus |
| KL | Kalmia latifolia |
| CF | Calycanthus floribus |

Section X6

Nantucket
August 2008 revised

0  2  4  6  8  10 m
1:100 Metric

269

Section X.06

x x — Amsonia hubrichtii

(Art) — Artemisia ludoviciana

◯ — Baptisia leucantha

x x x — Echinacea 'Rubinstern'

+ Echinacea 'Fatal Attraction'

∴ — Molinia 'Moorhexe'

+ Eragrostis spectabilis

∴ — Liatris spicata or Anaphalis margaritacea 65% +

◯ (Spo) — Sporobolus heterolepis                    Eragrostis spectabilis

| | |
|---|---|
| Acon | Aconitum wilsonii |
| Andro | Andropogon gerardii |
| Ane | Anemone 'Robustissima' |
| Ast VP | Astilbe 'Visions in Pink' |
| Ast umb | Aster umbellatus |
| Cal br | Calamagrostis brachytricha |
| Cal KF | Calamagrostis 'Karl Foerster' |
| Eup | Eupatorium maculatum 'Gateway' |
| Filip | Filipendula magnifica |
| Hel | Helenium 'Rubinzwerg' |
| Helian | Helianthus salicifolius |
| Macl | Macleaya cordata |
| Mon | Monarda fistulosa |
| Rheum | Rheum palmatum |
| Sorgh | Sorghastrum nutans |
| Stipa | Stipa gigantea |
| Thal | Thalictrum rochebruneanum |
| ◯ | Asclepias incarnata |
| ✳ | Miscanthus 'Malepartus' |

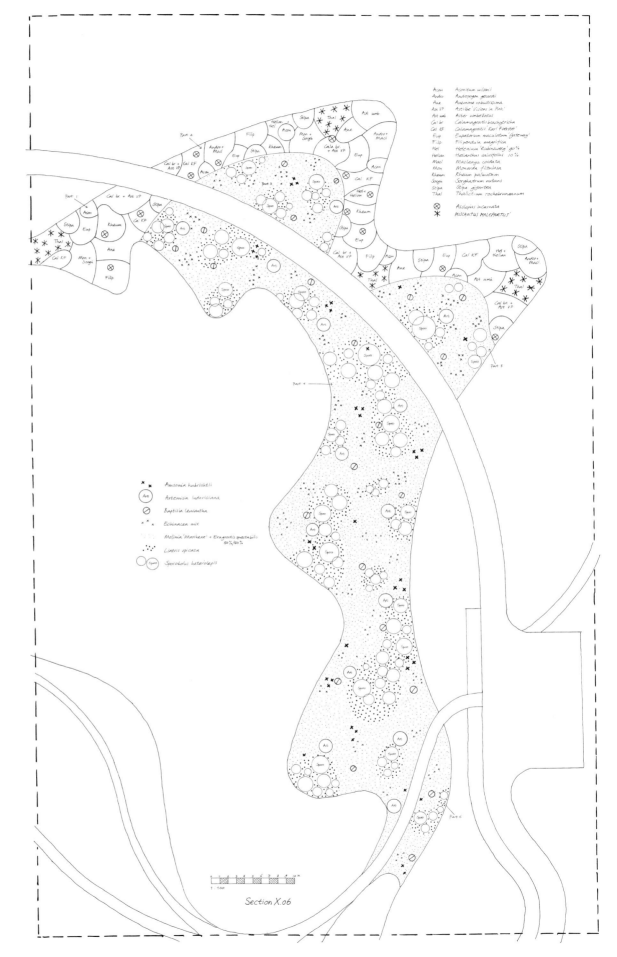

Acon    Aconitum wilsonii
Andro   Andropogon gerardii
Ane     Anemone robustissima
Ast VP  Astilbe 'Visions in Pink'
Ast umb Aster umbellatus
Cal br  Calamagrostis brachytricha
Cal KF  Calamagrostis 'Karl Foerster'
Eup     Eupatorium maculatum 'gateway'
Filip   Filipendula magnifica
Hel     Helenium 'Rubinzwerg' 90%
Helian  Helianthus salicifolius 10%
Macl    Macleaya cordata
Mon     Monarda fistulosa
Rheum   Rheum palmatum
Sorgh   Sorghastrum nutans
Stipa   Stipa gigantea
Thal    Thalictrum rochebruneanum

⊗  Asclepias incarnata
✳  MISCANTHUS MALEPARTUS

✶  Amsonia hubrichtii
Art  Artemisia ludoviciana
⊘  Baptisia leucantha
✗ ✗  Echinacea mix
Molinia 'Moorhexe' + Eragrostis spectabilis
        50%/60%
Liatris spicata
Sporo  Sporobolus heterolepis

Section X.06

271

# Photography Credits

Iwan Baan  189, 196–97, 198–99, 214–15
Alexandre Bailhache  260–61
Amy Barkow / Barkow Photo  220–21, 228
Nicola Browne  12, 33, 36–37, 38, 72–73, 81, 88–89, 170–71, 184
Imogen Checketts  119
Courtesy Emschergenossenschaft  54–55
Kurt Fortin  278–79
Andreas Grosse  21
Walter Herfst  34–35, 60–61, 62–63, 64–65, 98–99, 100–1, 178–79, 248–49
Erik Hesmerg  11, 16–17, 204–5, 212–13
Neil Holmes  115
Michael King  250–51, 252, 258, 259
Andrew Lawson  247
Marianne Majerus  79, 80, 253, 254
Courtesy Millennium Park, Inc. / Peggy Vagenius  166–67
Piet Oudolf  1, 26–27, 28–29, 31, 39, 42–43, 46–47, 48–49, 56–57, 69–70, 71
74, 75, 76–77, 78, 82, 90, 91, 96–97, 103, 106–7, 108–9, 110–11, 112–13,
116–17, 118, 125, 126–27, 129, 130, 131, 132, 133, 134, 135, 136, 137,
160–61, 162–63, 164–65, 172–73, 174–75, 176–77, 182, 183, 185, 186–87,
193–94, 195 all, 200–1, 202–3, 206–7, 208–9, 210–11, 217, 222–23, 224–25,
226–27, 229, 230–31, 236–37, 238–39, 242–43, 264–65, 272–73, 274–75, 276–77, 281
Sven Petterson  85
Sabrina Rothe  19, 20, 23
Jo Whitworth  83, 240–41, 244–45, 256–57
Rob Whitworth  255
Gregor C. Wolf / Bilderdienst Bonn  140–41, 142–43, 144–45, 146–47, 148
Herman Wouters  181

"He's gotten away from the soft pornography of the flower," said Charles Waldheim, the director of the landscape architecture program at the University of Toronto. "He's interested in the life cycle, how plant material ages over the course of the year," and how it relates to the plants around it. Like a good marriage, his compositions must work well together as its members age.

—New York Times, January 31, 2008